# Gross Negligence Manslaughter

## Placing legal restrictions pre-emptively on emerging autopoietic and intelligent computer systems.

**Mr Kristian Putman**

Cover Illustration By Ainars Strods

This book is independently published by Mr Kristian Putman.

Q5084961, Teesside University Mail Room, Middlesbrough Tower, Teesside University, Middlesbrough, Cleveland, TS13BA

ISBN: 9781096438366

**Gross negligence manslaughter – Placing legal restrictions pre-emptively on emerging autopoietic and intelligent computer systems.**

## Abstract

This research begins with an explanation of the fundamentals of Gross Negligence Manslaughter and Artificial Intelligence. This follows onto a discussion of various industries that employ Artificial Intelligence, and the problems that these industries could encounter from the perspective of the law on Gross Negligence Manslaughter. With an understanding of the fundamentals and the issues, chapter three then encompasses an analysis of potential solutions which could be utilised by the legislature, including the advantages and disadvantages of each. Finally, the research concludes with a recommendation for the best actions moving forward.

During the course of this research, legislation such as the Automated and Electronic Vehicles Act 2018 will be examined alongside cases such as R v Adomako [1994] 3 WLR 288 with the aim of assessing how each would interact with issues arising from the use of Intelligent Machines.

# Contents

## Acknowledgements

I would like to thank Annabelle James for putting up with my seemingly ridiculous questions, and for the direction that she provided when I needed it.

I would also like to thank Chris Noon for his criticisms of my layout and his perspective, which allowed me to see new avenues of thought that I had not previously considered.

It is more than necessary to also mention Harsimran Kaur, Shaywa Nzar, Joseph Potts, Cainan Lonsdale, Richard Walker and Lucy Thompson for their questions and opinions throughout my process, each of which allowed me to better assess both my legal and philosophical positions.

I swore to mention Lin from the library, after she issued Joseph Potts with a free student card and then charged him five pounds in late book fees. Which allowed me a very good chuckle.

In honour of F.D.C. Willard, I must not forget to credit E.M. Bagheera for his ever-critical gaze, quiet contemplation and company. Without which I may have lost my sanity at times.

Finally, thanks Danni.

# 1. Introduction of Concepts

The purpose of this dissertation is to examine the current legislation surrounding computer intelligence, autopoiesis and automation. This research will focus specifically on autopoietic[1] and intelligent computer systems[2] and the potential for such a system to kill, the research will then apply the current law on Gross Negligence Manslaughter (GNM)[3] in an attempt to determine whether a person should be held legally responsible[4] for a systems actions in the event that it does

---

[1] Humberto R Maturana and Francisco J Varela, *Autopoiesis and Cognition: The Realization of the Living* (1st edn, D Reidel Publishing Company 1980) 81; see also Rachel Herron, 'A social systems approach to understanding the racial effect of the section 44 counter-terror stop and search powers' [2015] 11(4) Int JLC 383

[2] Andreas Kaplan and Michael Haenlein, 'Siri, Siri, in my hand: Who's the fairest in the land? On the interpretations, illustrations, and implications of artificial intelligence' (2019) 62 Business Horizons 15; see also Emma L Flett and Jennifer F Wilson, 'Artificial intelligence: is Johnny 5 alive? Key bits and bytes from the UK's robotics and artificial intelligence inquiry' [2017] 23(3) CTLR 72

[3] Crown Prosecution Service, 'Homicide: Murder and Manslaughter' (Crown Prosecution Service, 19 February 2019) < https://www.cps.gov.uk/legal-guidance/homicide-murder-and-manslaughter> accessed 04 March 2019; see also Anne Lodge, 'Gross negligence manslaughter on the cusp: the unprincipled privileging of harm over culpability' [2017] 81(2) The Journal of Criminal Law 125

[4] George P Fletcher, *Rethinking Criminal Law* (Oxford University Press 2000) 398; see also Robert Wheeler, 'Gross negligence manslaughter: what does 'gross' entail?' (University Hospital Southampton, February 2018) <http://www.uhs.nhs.uk/HealthProfessionals/Clinical-law-updates/Gross-negligence-manslaughter-what-does-gross-entail.aspx> accessed 06 November 2018

take a life. The research will conclude with a discussion on how these systems could be legally restricted or regulated[5] to limit potential for loss of life.

The modern rules for determining GNM were described in *Adomako*,[6] which set out a four-step process for determining a defendant's guilt. *Adomako's* duty of care requirement[7] can be satisfied by either a criminal[8] or tort law duty of care.[9] *Donoghue*[10] set out the original neighbour test in tort law, which required proximity between the claimant and the respondent,[11] and reasonable foresight that the harm would occur.[12] The original neighbour test was later built on by *Caparo*[13] which, in addition to the proximity and foreseeability

---

[5] Westlaw UK, 'Health and safety: regulation and enforcement', Insight (26th June 2018) <Westlaw> accessed 04 March 2019; see also *Lauri Love v The National Crime Agency* [2019] 2 WLUK 464

[6] *R v Adomako* [1994] 3 WLR 288, 172; see also Norman Williams, 'Gross negligence manslaughter in healthcare: The report of a rapid policy review' (Gov.uk, 2018) <https://assets.publishing.service.gov.uk/government/uploads/system/uploads/attachment_data/file/717946/Williams_Report.pdf> accessed 05 March 2019, 11

[7] *Adomako* (n 6) 176

[8] Nature, 'Shock and law: The Italian system's contempt for its scientists' [2012] 490 Nature 446

[9] *Caparo Industries Plc. v Dickman and Others* [1990] 2 WLR 358

[10] *Donoghue v Stevenson* [1932] AC 562

[11] *Bourhill v Young* [1943] AC 92

[12] *Home Office v Dorset Yacht Co Ltd* [1970] 2 WLR 1140

[13] *Caparo* (n 9)

requirements, included the requirement that imposing a duty of care should be fair, just, and reasonable.[14]

Once a duty of care has been established between the complainant and the defendant,[15] it must be shown that there has been a legal breach of the established duty.[16] While the tort law duty of care can apply, the defence in tort law of *ex turpi causa*[17] or the illegality defence, cannot.[18] If the duty of care is found to have been breached, the first two requirements will have been satisfied, then it must be shown that the breach caused the death of the victim.[19] If the chain of causation was broken then the claim of GNM would not succeed.[20]

---

[14] *Hill v Chief Constable of West Yorkshire* [1989] AC 53, 60; see also Jenny Steele, *Tort Law: Text, Cases, and Materials* (3rd edn, Oxford University Press 2014) 163-165

[15] *Anns and Others v Merton London Borough Council* [1977] 2 WLR 1024, 734; see also *Gooda Walker Ltd (In Liquidation) and Others v Deeny and Others* [1994] 3 WLR 761, 150-151; cf *X v Bedfordshire* [1995] 2 AC 633; cf Ying Hui Tan, 'Law Report: Child in care cannot sue council: X (minors) v Bedfordshire County Council - Queen's Bench Division (Mr Justice Turner), 12 November 1993' (The Independent, 23 December 1993) <https://www.independent.co.uk/arts-entertainment/law-report-child-in-care-cannot-sue-council-x-minors-v-bedfordshire-county-council-queens-bench-1469142.html> accessed 05 March 2019

[16] *R v Evans* [2009] 1 WLR 1999

[17] Amir Khan v Muhammad Zubair Hussain [2019] CSOH 11, 24-40; see also Clark v Farley [2018] EWHC 1007 (QB); Gujra v Roath and another [2018] 1 WLR 3208, 5; Alan Reed, 'Ex turpi causa and gross negligence manslaughter' [2005] 69(2) Journal of Criminal Law 132; Alan Reed, 'Gross negligence manslaughter and illegal activity' [2005] 150 Criminal Law 1

[18] *R v Wacker* [2002] EWCA Crim 1944

[19] *Adomako* (n 6)

Finally, the defendants conduct must have been "so bad"[21] as to amount to a crime in the opinion of the jury. This final requirement was challenged by *Misra*[22] as a potential breach of Article 6[23] and 7[24] of the European Convention of Human Rights, but the Court of Appeal upheld the requirement. It was challenged because the defendants felt that the jury were allowed too much freedom to define the offence, and that this could circumvent their right to a fair trial.[25] They also questioned whether it was fair for a serious offence to lack the need for *mens rea*.[26]

The judge in *Rowley*[27] indicated a fifth requirement in the Adomako test,[28] requiring criminality, and was not satisfied that the care providers had met that requirement due to their state of mind.[29] *Rowley* also highlighted that

---

[20] *R v Connolly (Mark Anthony)* [2007] EWCA Crim 790, 34; see also *R v Paul Anthony Finlay* [2003] EWCA Crim 3868, 13

[21] *Adomako* (n 6) 177

[22] *R v Misra and Srivastava* [2005] 1 Cr App R 21

[23] Convention for the Protection of Human Rights and Fundamental Freedoms (European Convention on Human Rights, as amended) (ECHR) art 6

[24] ibid art 7

[25] Margaret Brazier and Amel Alghrani, 'Fatal medical malpractice and criminal liability' [2009] 25(2) PN 51; see also Lodge (n 3) 130

[26] *R v Lane and another* [2018] 1 WLR 3647, 3; see also *R v M (D) and another* [2011] 1 WLR 822, 1; *R v Johnson (Wayne)* [2018] 1 WLR 19, 7; *Garnett v State* 332 Md 571 (Md 1993) (US)

[27] *R (on the application of Rowley) v DPP* [2003] EWHC 693

[28] *Adomako* (n 6) 176

[29] *Rowley* (n 27) 28

actual foreseeability of harm was not a requirement in cases of GNM,[30] because Dr Adomako would have corrected the situation had he foreseen the harm. *Adomako*[31] was confirmed in *Jones*[32] and *Attorney General's Reference (No.2 of 1999)*.[33] The lack of requirement for actual foreseeability is an important consideration in instances involving learning machines and their creators due to their potential to act unexpectedly.[34]

In 1936, Turing theorised a universal computing machine in his paper 'On computable numbers, with an application to the entscheidungsproblem'.[35] Turing described a machine which could be used to "compute any computable sequence",[36] at this point in his writings it is unclear whether the idea of an intelligent machine[37] had formed itself as a possibility, but it is clear that Turing had built heavily upon the work of Lovelace, who had worked

---

[30] ibid 29

[31] *Adomako* (n 6)

[32] *R v DPP Ex p. Jones (Timothy)* [2000] IRLR 373

[33] *Attorney General's Reference (No.2 of 1999)* [2000] QB 796

[34] Joel Lehman and others, 'The Surprising Creativity of Digital Evolution: A Collection of Anecdotes from the Evolutionary Computation and Artificial Life Research Communities' [2018] Cornell University Neural and Evolutionary Computing arXiv:1803.03453v1 <https://arxiv.org/abs/1803.03453v1> accessed 05 March 2019

[35] Alan M Turing, 'On computable numbers, with an application to the entscheidungsproblem' [1936] 42(1) Proceedings of the London Mathematical Society 230

[36] ibid 241

[37] Alan M Turing, 'Computing Machinery and Intelligence' [1950] 49 Mind 433

extensively on the Babbage Engine.[38] Lovelace expressed scepticism in her notes that a machine could ever do anything more than perform procedural operations and complete basic mathematical problems.[39]

Turing advanced his ideas in a paper titled 'Computing Machinery and Intelligence',[40] which developed the basic idea behind an intelligent or conscious computer. In the present day, standard home computers[41] are now capable of feats such as Natural Language Processing[42] (the ability for a machine to take a language input such as English and output a coherent response)[43] which in 1936

---

[38] James Essinger, *Ada's Algorithm: How lord Byron's Daughter Launched the Digital Age* (Gibson Square 2013) 95; see also Charles Babbage, *Passages from The life of a Philosopher* (Longman, Green, Longman, Roberts & Green 1864) 41-67; Bruce Collier and James MacLachlan, *Charles Babbage and the Engines of Perfection* (Oxford University Press 1998) 104

[39] Ursula Martin, 'Ada Lovelace and the abstract machine' (The Times Literary Supplement, 11th October 2016) <https://www.the-tls.co.uk/articles/public/ada-lovelaces-abstract-machine/> accessed 05 March 2019

[40] Turing (n 37)

[41] Sandro Villinger, 'How powerful a computer do you really need?' (AVG, 16th July 2018) <https://www.avg.com/en/signal/how-powerful-a-computer-do-you-really-need> accessed 05 March 2019

[42] Jacob Devlin and Ming-Wei Chang, 'Open Sourcing BERT: State-of-the-Art Pre-training for Natural Language Processing' (Google AI Blog, 2nd November 2018) <https://ai.googleblog.com/2018/11/open-sourcing-bert-state-of-art-pre.html> accessed 13 November 2018

[43] Vyas Ajay Bhagwat, 'Deep Learning for Chatbots' (2018) San Jose University Masters Projects <https://scholarworks.sjsu.edu/cgi/viewcontent.cgi?article=1645&context=etd_projects> accessed 05 March 2019

could have been considered science fiction. Turing coined the "Turing Test"[44] in his latter paper where he suggested that to pass an intelligence test a computer would only need to convince an interrogator to believe that it was intelligent.[45]

The Computer Misuse Act (CMA)[46] goes some way towards punishing criminals that use computers in nefarious ways,[47] but a potential modern-day issue with the Act is that it views computers as tools.[48] Section 1(1)

---

[44] Turing (n 37) 1; see also Larry J Crockett, *The Turing Test and the Frame Problem: AI's Mistaken Understanding of Intelligence* (Ablex Publishing Corporation 1994)

[45] Crockett (n 44) 94; see also cf Crockett (n 44) 146; Robert Epstein, *Parsing the Turing Test: Philosophical and Methodological Issues in the Quest for the Thinking Computer* (Springer 2008) xiii; B Jack Copeland, *Alan Turing's Automatic Computing Engine: The Master Codebreaker's Struggle to Build the Modern Computer* (Oxford University Press 2005) 125

[46] Computer Misuse Act 1990

[47] *Love v Government of the United States of America (Liberty intervening)* [2018] 1 WLR 2889, 7; see also *McKinnon v Government of the United States of America* [2008] 1 WLR 1739; *Various Claimants v Wm Morrison Supermarkets plc* [2019] 2 WLR 99, 13; *R v Connor Douglas Allsopp* [2019] EWCA Crim 95, 2; *Love (n 5)*; *Privacy International v Secretary of State for Foreign and Commonwealth Affairs* [2016] HRLR 21, 46; *R v Mudd* [2017] EWCA Crim 1395, H2

[48] *Christian Connor v Regina* [2019] EWCA Crim 234, 4; see also *Allsopp* (n 47), 7; *In the Matter of Kent County Council v [Adult A], [Adult B], [Adult C], [Adult D]* [2017] WL 06806128, 95; *Cantor Fitzgerald International v Tradition (UK) Ltd & Ors* [1999] WL 1048259; Mark A Gluck and Catherine E Myers, *Gateway to Memory: An Introduction to Neural Network Modeling of the Hippocampus and Learning* (A Bradford Book 2001) 3-4; Jesse Miller, 'Computer Tools | Computer Features & Benefits' (streetdirectory.com, 2019) <https://www.streetdirectory.com/travel_guide/136883/computers/computer_tools__computer_features__benefits.html> accessed 05 March 2019

states "a person is guilty of an offence..."[49] which is common wording within legislation created by Parliament but fails to take into account modern advances[50] where a computer might decide to access computer material in an unauthorised way without explicit direction.[51] At the time the Act came into force, twenty-eight years ago, many computers contained 32-bit processors with 16-bit data busses operating at speeds of 16MHz.[52]

The average home computer in 2018, for instance, could contain a 64-bit processor with eighteen physical cores[53] operating at 4.4GHz.[54] This means that a computer

---

[49] CMA (n 46) S1

[50] !MEDIENGRUPPE BITNIK, 'Random DarkNet Shopper' (!MEDIENGRUPPE BITNIK, 14th October 2014) <https://wwwwwwwwwwwwwwwwwwwwww.bitnik.org/r/> accessed 28 February 2018; see also Aatif Sulleyman, 'Google AI creates its own 'Child' AI that's more advanced than Systems built by Humans' (The Independent, 5th December 2017) <https://www.independent.co.uk/life-style/gadgets-and-tech/news/google-child-ai-bot-nasnet-automl-machine-learning-artificial-intelligence-a8093201.html> accessed 13 November 2018

[51] George Seif, 'AutoKeras: The Killer of Google's AutoML' (Towards Data Science, 31st July 2018) <https://towardsdatascience.com/autokeras-the-killer-of-googles-automl-9e84c552a319> accessed 05 March 2019

[52] Appendix A

[53] Max Domeika, Software Development for Embedded Multi-core Systems: A Practical Guide Using Embedded Intel ® Architecture (Elsevier 2008) 57-59; see also James Reinders, Intel Threading Building Blocks Outfitting C++ for Multi-Core Processor Parallelism (O'Reilly Media 2007) XV; Margaret Rouse, 'multi-core processor' (TechTarget, August 2013) <https://searchdatacenter.techtarget.com/definition/multi-core-processor> accessed 06 March 2019

[54] Appendix A

today could perform eighteen operations, up to sixty-four binary[55] digits in length, four-billion-four-hundred-million (short scale)[56] times per second. In other words, computers today can compute numbers over one-hundred-and-forty-billion (long scale billion, short scale trillion)[57] times larger and two-thousand-four-hundred times faster, than a computer from 1990. Which illustrates an increase in speed[58] which has had a drastic impact on where and how modern computers are being utilised by members of society within day to day life.

Placing these numbers into perspective, a person using 10%[59] of their brain's neurons,[60] with a brain identical to the brain listed in Appendix A, would be able to perform

---

[55] Tariq Jamil, *Complex Binary Number System: Algorithms and Circuits* (Springer 2013) vii; David M Gay, *Correctly Rounded Binary-Decimal and Decimal-Binary Conversions* (AT&T Bell Laboratories 1990)

[56] Alexis Ulrich, 'Long and short numeric scales' (Of Language and Numbers, 24th August 2013) <https://www.languagesandnumbers.com/articles/en/long-and-short-numeric-scales/> accessed 30 November 2018

[57] ibid

[58] David Deutsch, 'Quantum theory, the Church-Turing principle and the universal quantum computer' (1985) A 400 Proceedings of the Royal Society of London 97, 15

[59] Claudia Hammond, 'Do we only use 10% of our brains?' (BBC Future, 13th November 2012) <http://www.bbc.com/future/story/20121112-do-we-only-use-10-of-our-brains> accessed 30 November 2018

[60] Peter Dayan and LF Abbott, *Theoretical Neuroscience* (The MIT Press 2001) 1.1; see also Chris Eliasmith and Charles H Anderson, *Computational Neuroscience: Computation, Representation and Dynamics in Neurobiological Systems* (The MIT Press 2003) 9-11

at 86GHz on average. An Intel Core i9 7980XE processor, identical to the one listed in Appendix A, would be able to perform at 79.2GHz. The myth that human beings only use 10% of their brain has been proven false,[61] however with multiple i9 processors working together,[62] their combined speed could exceed the Appendix A human brain. Although many more processors may be needed to compete with a non-discrete state system.[63]

The importance of this information lies in the sheer scale of advancement,[64] the law has not significantly advanced its view of computers in the past thirty years.[65] Meanwhile the modern-day computer has now evolved significantly in comparison to the computers that were originally legislated on in 1990.[66] The human brains rate of evolution[67] is slowly being surpassed by scientific

---

[61] Hammond (n 59)

[62] Domeika (n 53) 5

[63] H Ahmed and P J Spreadbury, *Analogue and digital electronics for engineers: An Introduction* (Cambridge University Press 1984) 254-259; see also Grahame Smillie, *Analogue and Digital Communication Techniques* (Elsevier Science 1999) 59-96; R S Soin, F Maloberti and J Franca, *Analogue To Digital ASICs: circuit techniques, design tools and applications* (Peter Peregrinus 1991) 213-237

[64] Jon Katz, 'Did Gates really say 640k is enough for anyone?' (Wired, 16th January 1997) <https://www.wired.com/1997/01/did-gates-really-say-640k-is-enough-for-anyone/> accessed 06 March 2019

[65] Appendix B

[66] ibid

[67] Russell Howard Tuttle, 'Human evolution' (Encyclopaedia Britannica, 8th January 2019) <https://www.britannica.com/science/human-evolution> accessed 06 March 2019; see also National Museum of natural History, 'Bigger

advancements in computer technology which have maintained the trajectory described by Gordon Moore ("Moore's Law").[68] Moore, who co-founded Intel,[69] stated that the number of transistors in an integrated circuit roughly doubles every two years.[70] Many have expressed concern over this phenomenon.[71]

The law is shifting slowly with the introduction of new legislation such as the Automated and Electric Vehicles Act 2018 (AEVA),[72] which received Royal Assent on the 19th July 2018.[73] The AEVA[74] bears similar problems to the CMA[75] by virtue of the fact that it is a

---

Brains: Complex Brains for a Complex World' (Smithsonian Institution, 6th March 2019) <http://humanorigins.si.edu/human-characteristics/brains> accessed 06 March 2019

[68] Gordon E. Moore, 'Cramming More Components onto Integrated Circuits' (1965) 38(8) Electronics 114

[69] Intel, 'Intel at 50: Gordon Moore on the Founding of Intel' (Intel News Byte, 2nd July 2018) <https://newsroom.intel.com/news/intel-50-gordon-moore-founding-intel/> accessed 30 November 2018

[70] Moore (n 68)

[71] Aatif Sulleyman, 'AI is highly likely to destroy humans, Elon Musk warns' (The Independent, 24th November 2017) <https://www.independent.co.uk/life-style/gadgets-and-tech/news/elon-musk-artificial-intelligence-openai-neuralink-ai-warning-a8074821.html> accessed 08 October 2018; see also Rory Cellan-Jones, 'Stephen Hawking warns artificial intelligence could end mankind' (BBC, 2nd December 2014) <https://www.bbc.co.uk/news/technology-30290540> accessed 08 October 2018

[72] Automated and Electric Vehicles Act 2018

[73] Parliament, 'Bill documents — Automated and Electric Vehicles Act 2018' (Parliament, 19th July 2018) <https://services.parliament.uk/bills/2017-19/automatedandelectricvehicles/documents.html> accessed 06 March 2019

[74] AEVA (n 72)

response to the symptoms of technological advancement and does not address the core issue of computer intelligence or learning.[76] The contents of the act centres on the responsibility for insurance and general liability. Section 2(7) of the AEVA[77] does illustrate that Parliament has considered the potential liability of others, possibly including software programmers.

Sections 4[78] and 5[79] of the AEVA suggest this also, because they mention "software updates" and discuss the "safety-critical" nature of certain updates which clearly indicates an awareness of the problems that could arise through the implementation of dangerous software.[80] This awareness is a good first step towards a more complete

---

[75] CMA (n 46)

[76] Dario Amodei and others, 'Concrete Problems in AI Safety' (2016) Google Brain <https://arxiv.org/pdf/1606.06565.pdf> accessed 01 February 2018; see also University of Chicago, 'Fundamental Issues in Machine Learning' (2009) The University of Chicago <https://ttic.uchicago.edu/~pengjian/MLCourse/intro.pdf> accessed 06 March 2019; iPullRank, 'Machine Learning for Marketers: A Comprehensive Guide to Machine Learning' (2017) iPullRank <https://assets.ctfassets.net/j5zy0n17n2ql/2D4mX8PjV6iC6i8cIuSCwk/23a4eb b99a6e9d5a82b2f03e1262f39d/ml-whitepaper.pdf> accessed 06 March 2019

[77] AEVA (n 72) S2(7)

[78] AEVA (n 72) S4

[79] ibid S5

[80] Brent Kesler, 'The Vulnerability of Nuclear Facilities to Cyber Attack' [2011] 10(1) Strategic Insights 15; see also Kim Zetter, *Countdown to Zero Day: Stuxnet and the Launch of the World's First Digital Weapon* (Crown, 2014) 39-48; James P Farwell and Rafal Rohozinski, 'Stuxnet and the Future of Cyber War' (2011) 53(1) Survival 23

array of legislation on hardware and software that poses a potential threat to the public,[81] but future legislation on the matter should perhaps be less reactionary as this could impair the courts ability to act in certain foreseeable situations.[82] The Act[83] itself does not sufficiently address the criminal responsibility.

The current view of non-human intelligence[84] taken by the courts in England most closely resembles the opinion of Descartes,[85] with regards to intelligent machines.[86] Descartes believed that consciousness[87] and intelligence[88] were both products of the soul,[89] and that a

---

[81] ibid

[82] Hod Lipson and Melba Kurman, *Driverless: Intelligent Cars and the Road Ahead* (1st edn, MIT Press 4th October 2016); see also Vincent C Müller, *Risks of Artificial Intelligence* (1st edn, Chapman and Hall/CRC 10th December 2015)

[83] AEVA (n 72)

[84] Sara J Shettleworth, *Cognition, Evolution, and Behavior* (2nd edn, Oxford University Press 2010) 8-10

[85] René Descartes, *Discourse on Method of Rightly Conducting One's Reason and of Seeking Truth in the Sciences* (CreateSpace Independent Publishing Platform, 14th July 2017) 80

[86] Kaplan (n 2); see also Flett (n 2); Richard E Neapolitan and Xia Jiang, *Artificial Intelligence: With an introduction to Machine Learning* (2nd edn, CRC Press 2018) 2-8

[87] Shettleworth (n 84) 6-8; see also Shettleworth (n 84) 23-25; John R Searle, *Consciousness and Language* (Cambridge University Press 2002) 7-17; John R Searle, *The Mystery of Consciousness* (The New York Review of Books 1997) 3-18; G William Farthing, *The Psychology of Consciousness* (Prentice Hall 1992) 1-2

[88] Kaplan (n 2); see also Flett (n 2); Neapolitan (n 86); Shettleworth (n 84);

[89] *The King James Bible* (1611) 1 Thessalonians 5:23; See also *The Quran* 29:57; Peter S Eardley and Carl N Still, *Aquinas: A Guide for the Perplexed* (Bloomsbury 2010) 34-37; Tim Crane and Sarah Patterson, *History of the Mind-*

machine could never have these things, limited to producing results based on the disposition of their organs.[90] This is termed 'dualism'.[91] While the courts may no longer come to their decisions from a theological standpoint,[92] the opinion that anything non-human cannot be equal to a human in the eyes of the law does still bear a strong intimation of theological teachings.[93]

Ford discussed this concept of personhood and makes the point that in certain instances it is morally preferable to draw a hard line between persons and non-persons where only the former are the subject of moral obligations and the latter are exempt,[94] this discussion is used by Ford in the context of a person's right to die[95] but

*Body Problem* (Routledge 2000) 34-56; Ronald Polansky, *Aristotle's De Anima* (Cambridge University Press 2007) 188-199; Lucrezia Iris Martone, *Giamblico De Anima I frammenti la dottrina* (Pisa University Press 2014) 65-66

[90] Max Velmans, *Understanding Consciousness* (1st edn, Routledge 11th September 2002) 10; see also Descartes (n 85) 39

[91] William R Uttal, *Dualism: The Original Sin of Cognitivism* (Lawrence Erlbaum Associates 2004) 197-204; see also Patterson (n 89); Descartes (n 85)

[92] E A Livingstone, *The Oxford Dictionary of the Christian Church* (3rd edn, Oxford University Press 1997) 1478

[93] Aaron S Gross, 'Religion and Animals' (2017) Oxford Handbooks Online <http://www.oxfordhandbooks.com/view/10.1093/oxfordhb/9780199935420.001.0001/oxfordhb-9780199935420-e-10?print=pdf> accessed 07 March 2019

[94] Mary Ford, 'The Personhood Paradox and the 'Right to Die'' [2005] 13(1) Med L Rev 80, 1

[95] James E Thornton and Earl R Winkler, *Ethics and Aging: The Right to Live, The Right to Die* (The University of British Columbia 1988) 25-26; see also Lisa Yount, *Right to Die and Euthanasia* (Infobase 2007) 81; Raymond Whiting, *A Natural Right to Die: Twenty-Three Centuries of Debate* (Greenwood Press

can easily be applied to problems involving the recognition of non-human intelligence[96] in law. Interestingly, Ford hints that the terms 'human being' and 'person' are not always synonymous,[97] which suggests that one of these concepts perhaps extends further than the other allows.[98]

The legal standpoint that non-human intelligence should not or could not be recognised in law[99] is not unique to the law of England and Wales.[100] This is evident from

2002) 66; Jared Stark, *A Death of One's Own: Literature, Law, and the Right to Die* (Northwestern University Press 2018) 4; Howard Ball, *The Right to Die: A Reference Handbook* (ABC-CLIO 2017) 59-80; Marjorie B Zucker, *A Documentary History: The Right to Die Debate* (Greenwood Press 1999) 18; Martin D Carcieri, *Applying Rawls in the Twenty-First Century: Race, Gender, The Drug War and the Right to Die* (Palgrave Macmillan 2015) 87-102; Barry Rosenfield, *Assisted Suicide And The Right To Die: The Interface of Social Science, Public Policy, and Medical Ethics* (American Psychology Association 2004) 8; Michael DeCasare, *Death on Demand: Jack Kevorkian and the Right to Die Movement* (Rowman and Littlefield 2015) 101; Scott Cutler Shershow, *Deconstructing Dignity A Critique of the Right-to-Die Debate* (The University of Chicago Press 2014) 85-97; BA Rich, 'Personhood, patienthood, and clinical practice: Reassessing advance directives' (1998) 4 Psychology, Public Policy and Law 610

[96] cf *Naruto v Slater*, No. 16-15469 (9th Cir 2018); see also Kaplan (n 2); Flett (n 2); Neapolitan (n 86); Shettleworth (n 84);

[97] Michael Lacewing, 'Are all humans persons?' (Routledge, 16th November 2012) <http://cw.routledge.com/textbooks/alevelphilosophy/data/AS/Persons/Arehumanspersons.pdf> accessed 08 March 2019

[98] Ford (n 94); see also Lacewing (n 97)

[99] Jiahong Chen and Paul Burgess, 'The boundaries of legal personhood: how spontaneous intelligence can problematise differences between humans, artificial intelligence, companies and animals' (March 2019) Artificial Intelligence and Law 27(1), 73-92

[100] Union with England Act 1707; see also Government of Wales Act 2006

cases such as *Naruto*[101] where a United States court ruled that a Crested Macaque (monkey) could not hold copyright to works that it had produced. The court in this case did not rule that the monkey was not intelligent or conscious[102] but instead the court decided that it could not hold the copyright because statutory provisions[103] did not expressly permit an "animal"[104] to bring this type of claim before the courts.

Many scientists and philosophers have attempted to define intelligence and consciousness;[105] some have

---

[101] *Naruto* (n 96)

[102] *Naruto* (n 96); see also Andrés Guadamuz, 'The monkey selfie: copyright lessons for originality in photographs and internet jurisdiction' [2016] 5(1) Internet Policy Review 1; Andrés Guadamuz, 'Can the monkey selfie case teach us anything about copyright law?' (World Intellectual Property Magazine, February 2018) <https://www.wipo.int/wipo_magazine/en/2018/01/article_0007.html> accessed 10 March 2019; Scott Graham, 'No Standing for Monkey to Bring Selfie Copyright Suit' (The Recorder, 23rd April 2018) <https://www.law.com/therecorder/2018/04/23/no-standing-for-monkey-to-bring-selfie-copyright-suit/?slreturn=20190209214241> accessed 10 March 2019

[103] 17 USC §101-1401 (1976)

[104] *Naruto* (n 96); see also ibid

[105] Kevin Warwick, *Artificial Intelligence: The Basics* (1st edn, Routledge 1st March 2013) 17; see also Oxford University Press, *Oxford Advanced Learner's Dictionary* (8th edn, Oxford University Press 21st August 2012) 823; Howard Gardner, *Frames of Mind: The theory of multiple intelligences* (2nd edn, Basic Books 1993) XXVIII; Kirsi Tirri and Petri Nokelainen, *Measuring Multiple Intelligences and Moral Sensitivities in Education* (Sense Publishers 2011) 122; Robert J Sternberg and James C Kaufman, *The Evolution of Intelligence* (Lawrence Erlbaum Associates 2002) IX; Jean Piaget, *The Psychology of Intelligence* (Armand Colin 1947) 7-8; Aleksandr Romanovich Luria, *Cortical*

narrowed their attempts to human intelligence and consciousness[106] while others have attempted to define the terms in their broader or universal sense.[107] Warwick's broad definition of intelligence is "[T]he variety of information processing processes that collectively enable a being to autonomously pursue its survival."[108] The Oxford Advanced Learner's Dictionary (OALD) definition is "[T]he ability to learn, understand and think in a logical way about things; the ability to do this well."[109] Either of these definitions could be adopted by the courts but the ambiguity would be problematic.[110]

---

*Functions in Man* (Basic Books 1966); Paul Wood and Paul Englert, 'Intelligence Compensation Theory: A Critical Examination of the Negative Relationship Between Conscientiousness and Fluid and Crystallised Intelligence' (2009) 2 The Australian and New Zealand Journal of Organisational Psychology 19; Albert Bandura, 'Perceived Self-Efficacy in Cognitive Development and Functioning' (1993) 28(2) Educational Psychologist 117; Phillip L Ackerman and Margaret E Beier, 'Intelligence, Personality, and Interests in the Career Choice Process' (2003) 11(2) Journal of Career Assessment 205; Rex E Jung and Richard J Haier, 'The Parieto-Frontal Integration Theory (P-FIT) of intelligence: Converging neuroimaging evidence' (2007) 30(2) Behavioral and Brain Sciences 135; Loes van Aken and others, 'Representation of the Cattell–Horn–Carroll Theory of Cognitive Abilities in the Factor Structure of the Dutch-Language Version of the WAIS-IV' (2017) 24(4) Assessment 458; Stuart J Ritchie, Tucker-Drob and Elliot M, 'How much does education improve intelligence? A meta-analysis' [2018] Psychological Science 29(8), 1358-1369; Amos E Dolbear, 'An Educational Allegory' [1899] Journal of Education 50(14), 235

[106] Gardner (n 105); see also cf Warwick (105); cf Dolbear (n 105)

[107] Warwick (n 105); see also Dolbear (n 105); cf Tirri (n 105)

[108] Warwick (n 105)

[109] OALD (n 105)

[110] Kent Greenawalt, *Statutory and Common Law Interpretation* (Oxford

These two definitions for intelligence contain various requirements for something to be considered intelligent. Warwick's definition[111] requires a variety of processes, a being and the pursuit of survival based on decisions made by those processes which in turn are based on information that they have processed collectively. The OALD definition[112] requires learning, understanding and thinking in a logical manner. The contrasting point between the two definitions is the number of things that could satisfy intelligence if each were to become the legal definition for intelligence. Finding a definition that could be adopted by the courts to determine intelligence is difficult.[113]

Thought experiments[114] such as John Searle's Chinese Room Argument[115] could be used to suggest that a computer cannot be determined to understand a concept purely based on observed actions,[116] this argument can also be used to suggest that human beings lack understanding for the same reasons. Searle's argument has merit when considered from the perspective of a fixed

---

University Press 2013) 76-77
[111] Warwick (n 105)
[112] OALD (n 105)
[113] Wood (n 105); see also Warwick (n 105)
[114] John R Searle, 'Minds, Brains, and Programs' [1980] 3(3) Behavioral and Brain Sciences 417; see also Erwin Schrödinger, 'Die gegenwärtige Situation in der Quantenmechanik' (1935) 23(48) Naturwissenschaften 807
[115] Searle (n 114)
[116] ibid

point in time, but his argument fails to consider where a person is given Chinese examples and learns to interpret them over a period of time;[117] such as could be the case with an 'intelligent' person or an Artificial Neural Network (ANN).[118]

Learning could be defined as changing in a logical way to better solve a problem based on experience. The ability to learn, in this sense, has already been demonstrated in machines,[119] with the development of ANNs,[120] which are an attempt to replicate the structure of a brain within a computer, literally digital neurons.[121] Success in this area of research has led to developments such as AlphaGo[122] which defeated the world champion in

---

[117] Stanford Encyclopaedia of Philosophy, 'The Chinese Room Argument' (Stanford Encyclopaedia of Philosophy, 19th March 2004) <https://plato.stanford.edu/entries/chinese-room/#4> accessed 30 November 2018

[118] Amit Konar, *Artificial Intelligence and Soft Computing: Behavioural and Cognitive Modelling of the Human Brain* (1st edn, CRC Press 8th December 1999) 40

[119] Lehman (n 34)

[120] Zhigang Zeng and Jun Wang, *Advances in Neural Network Research and Applications* (Springer-Verlag Berlin Heidelberg 2010) 405-412; see also Gluck (n 48) XIII; Timothy Masters, *Practical Neural Network Recipes in C++* (Academic Press 1993) 165-169; Cornelius T Leondes, *Neural Network Systems Techniques and Applications: Control and Dynamic Systems* (Academic Press 1998) XV; Dave Anderson and George McNeill, 'A DACS State-of-the-Art Report: Artificial Neural Networks Technology' (20th August 1992) DACS <https://knn.es/Artificial%20Neural%20Network%20Technologies.pdf> accessed 11 March 2019

[121] ibid

[122] Alex Hern, 'Google's Go-playing AI still undefeated with victory over world

the Chinese game GO. AlphaGo[123] and its successor AlphaZero[124] were both developed by Google's DeepMind laboratory which still has many scientists attempting to develop the next intelligent machine.[125]

This type of software goes through repeated iterations[126] of learning, becoming better at a set task each time, for example AlphaGo became a world champion in the game GO[127] by playing the game against past versions of itself.[128] Learning also occurs at a rate far superior to human beings due to the virtual environment[129] and the calculation speeds illustrated in Appendix A. Less complex ANNs have been demonstrated learning to play racing games on commercially available computers,[130] and it

number one' (The Guardian, 25th May 2017) <https://www.theguardian.com/technology/2017/may/25/alphago-google-ai-victory-world-go-number-one-china-ke-jie> accessed 28 February 2018

[123] ibid; see also DeepMind, 'DeepMind' (DeepMind Technologies Limited, 2018) <https://deepmind.com/> accessed 28 February 2018

[124] Demis Hassabis and David Silver, 'AlphaGo Zero: Learning from scratch' (DeepMind, 18th October 2017) <https://deepmind.com/blog/alphago-zero-learning-scratch/> accessed 1 December 2018

[125] DeepMind (n 123)

[126] Parag C Pendharkara, James A Rodgerb and Girish H Subramanian, 'An empirical study of the Cobb–Douglas production function properties of software development effort' (2008) 50(12) Information and Software Technology 1181

[127] American GO Association, 'A Brief History of Go' (American GO Association, 2019) <http://www.usgo.org/brief-history-go> accessed 11 March 2019

[128] Hern (n 122)

[129] Virtual Box, 'Welcome to VirtualBox.org!' (VirtualBox, 26th September 2011) <https://www.virtualbox.org/manual/ch01.html> accessed 11 March 2019

could be difficult in the future to stop a person from using the same software to drive a remote controlled car.[131]

Proving human understanding is an issue that has been considered many times already in law, for example the concept of Gillick competence[132] applies where children are seeking medical treatment without the consent of their parents and the Sexual Offences Act (SOA)[133] sets the statutory age of sexual consent at sixteen.[134] The concept of giving consent usually relies on 'understanding'.[135] Consent cannot be given without a firm basis of understanding, and yet no scientific test currently exists to measure understanding nor do the courts have any way to

---

[130] Ian Millington, *Artificial Intelligence for Games* (1st edn, CRC Press 28th July 2006); see also Geogios N Yannakakis, 'Game AI revisited' [2012] Proceedings of the 9th conference on Computing Frontiers, 285-292; Mauro Comi, 'How to teach AI to play Games: Deep Reinforcement Learning' (Towards Data Science, 15th November 2018) <https://towardsdatascience.com/how-to-teach-an-ai-to-play-games-deep-reinforcement-learning-28f9b920440a> accessed 11 March 2019; Neil Slater, 'Creating a self learning Mario Kart game AI?' (AI Stackexchange, 5th October 2018) <https://ai.stackexchange.com/questions/8220/creating-a-self-learning-mario-kart-game-ai> accessed 11 March 2019

[131] Hod Lipson and Melba Kurman, *Driverless: Intelligent Cars and the Road Ahead* (1st edn, MIT Press 4th October 2016); see also Leondes (n 120)

[132] *Gillick v West Norfolk and Wisbech Area Health Authority and Department of Health and Social Security* [1985] 3 WLR 830

[133] Sexual Offences Act 2003

[134] ibid S9(1)(c)(i)

[135] SOA (n 133) S30(2)(b); see also Mental Health Act 1983 S57(2)(a); Children Act 1989 S1(3)(a); Corporation Tax Act 2010 S81(4); Pensions Act 2004 S5(1)(d); *Gillick* (n 132)

determine that the understanding of one is equal to the understanding of another.

Due to the lack of any precise way to confirm levels of understanding,[136] if one test to determine a minimum level of understanding can be completed by a human, an animal or a machine to the same standard then it can be argued that the human's understanding under this test should be considered equal to the machines understanding under this test.[137] The courts could decide to create a test where the first requirement was to be human,[138] but this would ultimately demonstrate a bias against machines and animals without logical or scientific basis; it would in a sense be nepotistic.[139]

Thought is measurable if defined as the processing of information, because the speed at which information is processed can be measured in hertz;[140] this synonymy

---

[136] *L (A Child)* [2019] WL 00937194, 52; see also *Regina (Medical Justice and others) v Secretary of State for the Home Department (Equality and Human Rights Commission intervening)* [2017] 4 WLR 198, 162; *NCC v PB (By her litigation friend the Official Solicitor), TB (By his litigation friend the Official Solicitor)* [2014] EWCOP 14

[137] Ronald Schleifer, Robert Con Davis and Nancy Mergler, *Culture and Cognition: The Boundaries of Literary and Scientific Inquiry* (Cornell University Press 1992) 43; see also Kaplan (n 2); Flett (n 2); Neapolitan (n 86)

[138] John King Gamble, 'Human-Centric International Law: A Model and a Search for Empirical Indicators' [2005] 14 Tulane Journal of International and Comparative Law 61; see also *Alcock and Others v Chief Constable of South Yorkshire Police* [1991] 3 WLR 1057, 347

[139] 5 USC §⊠3110 (2006)

[140] BIPM, 'SI Brochure: The International System of Units (SI) [8th edition,

also allows for comparisons to be drawn between the OALD definition[141] and Warwick's definition.[142] If a more human-centric definition were to be used then it could encounter the same problems as the concept of understanding, in that predetermining the failure[143] of a test by biasing the test in favour of another does not allow for a fair or impartial result.[144] This differs from an inability to apply a well-reasoned and impartial test to something inanimate.

Warwick's definition includes an element which is not considered by the OALD definition; the pursuit of survival.[145] This presents a problem for both computers and humans attempting to satisfy his definition.[146] If pursuit of survival is required for intelligence, then victims of suicide would be considered unintelligent,[147] for this reason

2006; updated in 2014]' (BIPM, 1st February 2001) <https://www.bipm.org/en/publications/si-brochure/second.html> accessed 13 March 2019; see also Appendix A

[141] Oxford (n 105)

[142] Warwick (n 105)

[143] cf Forfeiture Act 1982 S2

[144] ECHR (n 23); see also Human Rights Act 1998

[145] Warwick (n 105)

[146] ibid; see also Lawrence Rifkin, 'Is the Meaning of Your Life to Make Babies?' (Scientific American, 24th March 2013) <https://blogs.scientificamerican.com/guest-blog/is-the-meaning-of-your-life-to-make-babies/> accessed 13 March 2019

[147] Neel Burton, 'Can It Be Right to Commit Suicide?' (Psychology Today, 22nd May 2012) <https://www.psychologytoday.com/gb/blog/hide-and-seek/201205/can-it-be-right-commit-suicide> accessed 13 March 2019

the pursuit of survival should perhaps be substituted for the pursuit of an objective. Turing committed suicide in June 1954,[148] just four years after publishing "Computing Machinery and Intelligence",[149] following a conviction for indecency.[150] In an attempt to critique himself, his paper set out nine common objections to computer intelligence.[151]

The theological objection (TO)[152] is an objection from the perspective that consciousness is a product of man's immortal soul,[153] which it is said a machine can never possess. This dualist perspective[154] is the view taken by Descartes[155] and is also the presumed origin of the current view taken by the courts. The TO covers a range of assumptions from the idea that a deity must create intelligence for it to exist,[156] through to the assumption that souls must exist to experience and influence consciousness or intelligence, for it to be valid.[157] This can only be proven or disproven alongside religion.[158]

---

[148] David Leavitt, *The Man Who Knew Too Much: Alan Turing and the invention of computers* (1st edn, Weidenfeld & Nicolson 22nd January 2015) 5

[149] Turing (n 37)

[150] Leavitt (n 148) 268

[151] Turing (n 37) 443

[152] Turing (n 37) 443-444

[153] *Bible* (n 89); see also *Quran* (n 89)

[154] Uttal (n 91); see also Patterson (n 89); Descartes (n 85)

[155] Descartes (n 85)

[156] Turing (n 37) 443

[157] Bible (n 89); see also Quran (n 89)

[158] T Edward Damer, *Attacking Faulty Reasoning: A Practical Guide to Fallacy-Free Arguments* (6th edn, Wadsworth Cengage Learning 2009) 17; see also

The head in the sand objection dismisses the possibility of machine intelligence due to the hope that a thinking machine could not exist.[159] This is the narrow view taken by a select few that suggests that if an extreme outcome were to become a possibility then the consequences would be too dire to think about.[160] The idea that some things are best left unconsidered because

---

Ethan Siegel, 'Can Science Prove the Existence Of God?' (Forbes, 20th January 2017) <https://www.forbes.com/sites/startswithabang/2017/01/20/can-science-prove-the-existence-of-god/> accessed 14 March 2019; John Shook, 'Proving God's Existence Is Impossible So Stop Trying' (Centre for Enquiry, 16th November 2011) <https://centerforinquiry.org/blog/proving_gods_existence_is_impossible/> accessed 14 March 2019

[159] Turing (n 37) 444

[160] Nick Bostrom, 'The superintelligent will: Motivation and instrumental rationality in advanced artificial agents.' (2012) 22(2) Minds and Machines 71; see also Cellan-Jones (n 71); Sulleyman (n 71); Tanya Lewis, 'Don't Let Artificial Intelligence Take Over, Top Scientists Warn' (Live Science, 12th January 2015) <https://www.livescience.com/49419-artificial-intelligence-dangers-letter.html> accessed 15 March 2019; Nick Srnicek, '4 Reasons Why Technological Unemployment Might Really Be Different This Time' (Novara Media, 30th March 2015) <https://novaramedia.com/2015/03/30/4-reasons-why-technological-unemployment-might-really-be-different-this-time/> accessed 15 March 2019; Francesca Bria, 'The robot economy may already have arrived' (Open Democracy, 20th February 2016) <https://www.opendemocracy.net/en/can-europe-make-it/robot-economy-full-automation-work-future/> accessed 15 March 2019; Robert Skidelsky, 'Rise of the robots: what will the future of work look like?' (Guardian, 19th February 2013) <https://www.theguardian.com/business/2013/feb/19/rise-of-robots-future-of-work> accessed 15 March 2019; Oscar Williams-Grut, 'Robots will steal your job: How AI could increase unemployment and inequality' (Business Insider, 15th February 2016) <https://www.businessinsider.com/robots-will-steal-your-job-citi-ai-increase-unemployment-inequality-2016-2?r=UK&IR=T> accessed 15 March 2019

thinking about them would have no impact on the outcome.[161] This can be applied to the law because it could be suggested that parliament should not waste its time legislating on something which is inevitable.[162]

Mathematical objections[163] arise from evidence which suggests that there are some things that a formal axiomatic system[164] could never answer, this argument is in essence the argument that a computer could never create its own "truths" or think beyond its own limits,[165] and Turing himself came to disagree with this.[166] To simplify the argument further, if a computer were to be asked an

---

[161] Turing (n 37) 444; see also cf Daniel Silverstone and Joe Whittle, '"Forget it, Jake. It's Chinatown": the policing of Chinese organised crime in the UK' (2016) Pol J 89(1), 70-84; cf Steve Bullock, 'Brexit is not inevitable. These are the steps Parliament could take to halt it' (The London School of Economics and Political Science, 14th May 2018) <https://blogs.lse.ac.uk/brexit/2018/05/14/brexit-is-not-inevitable-these-are-the-steps-parliament-could-take-to-halt-it/> accessed 15 March 2019

[162] cf Bullock (n 161); see also cf Silverstone (n 161)

[163] Turing (n 37) 444-445; see also Gualtiero Piccinini, 'Alan Turing and the Mathematical Objection' (2003) 13(1) Minds and Machines 23-48; Jack Copeland, 'The Mathematical Objection: Turing, Gödel, and Penrose on the Mind' (2008) Donald Bren School of Information and Computer Sciences <https://www.ics.uci.edu/~welling/teaching/271fall09/Copeland---TheMathematicalObjection.pdf> accessed 15 March 2019

[164] Michael T Battista, 'Formal Axiomatic Systems and Computer-Generated Theorems' [1982] 75(3) The Mathematics Teacher 215, 252

[165] Ian Sample, "It's able to create knowledge itself': Google unveils AI that learns on its own' (Guardian, 18th October 2017) <https://www.theguardian.com/science/2017/oct/18/its-able-to-create-knowledge-itself-google-unveils-ai-learns-all-on-its-own> accessed 15 March 2019

[166] Piccinini (n 163); see also Copeland (n 163)

unanswerable question then it could not answer,[167] Turing stated that this was only relevant to the machines intelligence if an intelligent being would have been able to answer the question asked, which would not be the case.[168]

The argument from consciousness[169] is that a machine could never produce a work of art based on emotion such as a person could,[170] this objection is countered by the argument that it cannot be evidenced that a person can. Nagel suggested that qualia forms an essential requirement for consciousness,[171] and this has been broadly accepted by many.[172] Thus if it is possible to imagine what it is like to be something else,[173] then it is likely that it is conscious, or that it can subjectively be

---

[167] Donald C Clarke, 'How Do We Know When an Enterprise Exists? Unanswerable Questions and Legal Polycentricity in China' (2005) George Washington University Law School <https://scholarship.law.gwu.edu/cgi/viewcontent.cgi?referer=https://www.google.com/&httpsredir=1&article=1049&context=faculty_publications> accessed 15 March 2019

[168] Turing (n 37) 444-445

[169] Turing (n 37) 445-447; see also William Lane Craig and J P Moreland, *The Blackwell Companion to Natural Theology* (Wiley-Blackwell 2009) 282-343

[170] Turing (n 37); see also Peter Bradley, 'Turing Test and Machine Intelligence' (The Mind Project, 2002) <http://www.mind.ilstu.edu/curriculum/turing_machines/turing_test_and_machine_intelligence.php> accessed 01 December 2018

[171] Thomas Nagel, *Mortal Questions* (Cambridge University Press 1979) 165-180

[172] Stanley James, 'Philosophy of AI: David Chalmers and the Hard Problem of Consciousness' (Mindbuilding Seminar, University of Osnabrück, 2003)

[173] Nagel (n 171); see also James (n 172)

viewed as such.[174] In other words, this is another unproven, and possibly unprovable, objection.

Arguments from various disabilities[175] arise where it can be said that a machine cannot perform a task in the same way that a human can,[176] but this argument could be applied between two people to determine that one is intelligent and the other is not for ridiculous reasons, for example person A has no legs and is therefore less intelligent than person B because person B is capable of completing a 100m sprint.[177] Arguments from various disabilities is prohibited from being applied to people by virtue of the Equality Act[178] and yet it is commonly applied between people and machines.

Lady Lovelace's objection[179] suggests that machines are incapable of originality resulting from their inability to learn independently,[180] current technological advances are surpassing this argument such as in the case of NASNet, an artificial intelligence which was built by

---

[174] Turing (n 37) 446

[175] Turing (n 37) 447-450

[176] Michael Wheeler, 'Plastic Machines: Behavioural Diversity and the Turing Test' [2010] Kybernetes 39(3), 466-480

[177] Dolbear (n 105)

[178] Equality Act 2010

[179] Turing (n 37) 450-451

[180] BBC News, 'A Point of View: Will machines ever be able to think?' (BBC News, 13th October 2013) <https://www.bbc.co.uk/news/magazine-24565995> accessed 02 December 2018

another artificial intelligence named autoML.[181] The independence that Lovelace described assumes that machines rely on procedural programming,[182] or that they perform operations in sequence as instructed by a human, thus everything they produce must originate from the human programmer.[183] The development of object-oriented programming (OOP)[184] offers an argument against this view, OOP allows blocks of code to be combined in different ways.

An example might be code written for a class[185] defined as 'animal' which would then be used by the child

---

[181] Barret Zoph and others, 'Learning Transferable Architectures for Scalable Image Recognition' (2018) Arxiv <https://arxiv.org/pdf/1707.07012.pdf> accessed 15 March 2019; see also Barret Zoph and others, 'AutoML for large scale image classification and object detection' (Google AI Blog, 2nd November 2017) <https://ai.googleblog.com/2017/11/automl-for-large-scale-image.html> accessed 15 March 2019

[182] T Ishida, Y Sasaki and Y Fukuhara, 'Use of procedural programming languages for controlling production systems' [1991] IEEE <https://ieeexplore.ieee.org/stamp/stamp.jsp?tp=&arnumber=120848> accessed 15 March 2019; see also Kenny Eliason, 'Difference between Object-Oriented Programming and Procedural Programming Languages' (NeonBrand, 1st August 2013) <https://neonbrand.com/website-design/procedural-programming-vs-object-oriented-programming-a-review/> accessed 15 March 2019

[183] cf Sulleyman (n 50); see also cf Barret Zoph and others, 'Learning Transferable Architectures for Scalable Image Recognition' (2018) Arxiv <https://arxiv.org/pdf/1707.07012.pdf> accessed 15 March 2019

[184] Danny Poo, Derek Kiong and Swarnalatha Ashok, *Object-Oriented Programming and Java* (2nd edn, Springer 2008) 1; see also Hasin Hayder, *Object-Oriented Programming with PHP5* (Packt Publishing 2007) 10-18; Simon Kendal, *Object Oriented Programming using Java* (Ventus Publishing 2009) 50-69; Eliason (n 183)

classes 'mammal' and 'reptile' which would then each have their own child classes for multiple other animals. The programmer could programmatically describe how a set 'cat' class might interact with a set 'dog' class,[186] but once the first ten million random[187] cat classes are initiated within the program its impractical to predict how cat thirty will interact with dog eighty in the same way that it is impractical to attempt to predict[188] who may or may not commit murder tomorrow.

The conceptual originality in this sense is the lack of broad predictability.[189] Simplifying this argument, if a computer is instructed to choose a random number between one and ten,[190] while the human may have issued the instruction and while arguments against randomness can be considered,[191] it would be wrong to state that the

---

[185] Kendal (n 185) 102-108; see also Poo (n 185) 53-55

[186] Robert Lafore, *Object-Oriented Programming in C++* (4th edn, Sams Publishing 2002) 215-263

[187] Lafore (n 187) 289-290; see also Jason M Rubin, 'Can a computer generate a truly random number?' (MIT School of Engineering, 1st November 2011) <https://engineering.mit.edu/engage/ask-an-engineer/can-a-computer-generate-a-truly-random-number/> accessed 15 March 2019

[188] Hector Zenil, *A Computable Universe: Understanding and Exploring Nature as Computation* (World Scientific Publishing 2013) 381-398; see also Adam Conner-Simons and Rachel Gordon, 'Teaching machines to predict the future' (MIT News, 21st June 2016) <http://news.mit.edu/2016/teaching-machines-to-predict-the-future-0621> accessed 15 March 2019

[189] Zenil (n 189); see also Gordon (n 189)

[190] Lafore (n 187) 289-290; see also Stephen Randy Davis and Chuck Sphar, *C# 2005 For Dummies* (Wiley Publishing 2006) 358;

[191] John Earman, *A primer on Determinism* (D Reidel 1986) 4-22

human operator chose the number. Where it is not possible to state that the human programmer chose the number, even if the human programmer had taught the computer how to select a number as randomly as possible, it must be said that the computer chose the number.[192]

The argument from continuity in the nervous system[193] suggests that because the brain has analogue components and is a non-discrete state system,[194] a digital computer cannot truly "think" in the same way as an analogue person.[195] Turing disagreed with this on the basis that any digital system can effectively mimic an analogue system if given enough computing power.[196] This principle

---

[192] Appendix C; see also Robert Hart, 'If an AI creates a work of art, who owns the copyright?' (World Economic Forum, 16th August 2017) <https://www.weforum.org/agenda/2017/08/if-an-ai-creates-a-work-of-art-who-owns-the-copyright> accessed 16 March 2019; Andres Guadamuz, 'Artificial intelligence and copyright' (World Intellectual Property Organisation, October 2017) <https://www.wipo.int/wipo_magazine/en/2017/05/article_0003.html> accessed 16 March 2019

[193] Turing (n 37) 451-452

[194] Thomas Connelly, 'Sounding the argument against the Turing Test from continuity in the nervous system.' (Philosophy Online, 17th September 2018) <https://philosophyonline.blog/2018/09/17/sounding-the-argument-against-the-turing-test-from-continuity-in-the-nervous-system/> accessed 02 December 2018

[195] Amitava Basak, *Analogue electronic circuits and systems* (Cambridge University Press 1991) 101-107; see also Sean Gallagher, 'Gears of war: When mechanical analog computers ruled the waves' (ARS Technica, 18th March 2014) <https://arstechnica.com/information-technology/2014/03/gears-of-war-when-mechanical-analog-computers-ruled-the-waves/> accessed 19 March 2019

was somewhat proven by researchers at the Technische Universität Wien[197] who successfully recreated a neural system,[198] based on a biological organism,[199] within a computer program. Replicating a living organism within a digital system was a step forward for artificial intelligence.[200]

The argument from the informality of behaviour[201] suggests that any system governed by set laws can be predicted[202] and cannot therefore be intelligent, however this argument suggests that there are no such laws of behaviour governing the human system and Turing argues that simply because these laws have not been defined does not mean that they do not exist.[203] The argument stems from the assumption that no matter how many rules are written to describe a person's behaviour, they can always do something unexpected which does not fit the

---

[196] Turing (n 37) 451-452

[197] Mathias Lechner, Radu Grosu, Ramin M Hasani, 'Worm-level Control through Search-based Reinforcement Learning' (6th February 2018) Technische Universität Wien <https://www.tuwien.ac.at/en/news/news_detail/article/125597/> accessed 02 December 2018

[198] Alfredo Weitzenfeld, Michael Arbib and Amanda Alexander, *The Neural Simulation Language: A System for Brain Modelling* (Massachusetts Institute of Technology 2002) 1

[199] William B Wood, *The Nematode Caenorhabditis elegans* (Cold Spring Harbor Press 1988) 1

[200] Lechner (n 197)

[201] Turing (n 37) 452

[202] Stuart J Russell and others, *Artificial Intelligence: A Modern Approach* (3rd edn, Harlow Pearson Education cop. 2016) 1024-1026

[203] Turing (n 37) 452-453

rules, whereas a computer could not display that form of intelligence.[204]

Finally, Extra Sensory Perception[205] is the argument that human beings can just know things. This argument resembles that of the TO[206] and the courts have in the past considered the supernatural, an example of this is *Cummins*[207] where the courts stated that they could not rule on the possibility of the extra-terrestrial.[208] Few if any of the objections that Turing suggested have not been raised since his paper,[209] and none have prevailed to the point that science has categorically concluded that machines cannot be conscious or intelligent under the right circumstances, but neither has it been proven that they can.[210]

Autopoiesis is the ability for something to replicate and maintain itself,[211] these two features have been demonstrated independently in various projects.[212] Self-

---

[204] Caroline Eisner and Martha Vicinus, *Originality, Imitation, and Plagiarism: Teaching Writing in the Digital Age* (The University of Michigan 2008)

[205] Turing (n 37) 453

[206] Turing (n 37) 443

[207] *Cummins v Bond* [1927] 1 Ch 167

[208] ibid, 175

[209] Turing (n 37)

[210] Malay Haldar, 'Did Turing Prove Machines Will Never Equal Humans?' (A Medium Corporation, 09 January 2016) <https://medium.com/technology-invention-and-more/did-turing-prove-machines-will-never-equal-humans-d73019b74a55> accessed 05 April 2019

[211] Maturana (n 1) 88-95

replication in biology comes generally in two broad forms, asexual[213] and sexual[214] reproduction, the former of which has partially moved into the field of Computer Science (CS) in the form of Quines.[215] In 2018, Chang and Lipson produced a paper detailing how this could be done with ANNs.[216] Although in theory both can be simulated in software and hardware,[217] there are few clear examples of hardware that produces copies of itself,[218] software replication occurs constantly however, with computer viruses.[219]

Since the only resource a computer really needs to function is electricity,[220] solar panels have now been

---

[212] Nelson Fernandez, Carlos Maldonado, Carlos Gershenson, 'Information Measures of Complexity, Emergence, Self-organization, Homeostasis, and Autopoiesis' (Univesidad de Pamplona, 31st July 2013)

[213] Jan Engelstädter, 'Asexual but Not Clonal: Evolutionary Processes in Automictic Populations' [2017] 206(2) GENETICS 993

[214] Sarah P Otto and Thomas Lenormand, 'Resolving the paradox of sex and recombination' [2002] 3 Nature Reviews Genetics 252

[215] Paul Bratley and Jean Millo, 'Computer recreations' [1972] Software Practice and Experience 2,397-400

[216] Oscar Chang and Hod Lipson, 'Neural Network Quine' (Columbia University, 24th May 2018)

[217] Chang (n 216); see also Bratley (n 215); Robert A Freitas and Ralph C Merkle, *Kinematic Self-Replicating Machines* (Landes Bioscience 2004) 1

[218] Freitas (n 217)

[219] CISCO, 'What Is the Difference: Viruses, Worms, Trojans, and Bots?' (Cisco Systems, 14th June 2018) <https://www.cisco.com/c/en/us/about/security-center/virus-differences.html#3> accessed 06 April 2019

[220] Chris Woodford, 'Computers' (ExplainThatStuff, 25th December 2019) <https://www.explainthatstuff.com/howcomputerswork.html> accessed 06 April 2019

coupled with software and robotics to create computers that consume sunlight autonomously in pursuit of their own survival, this was eloquently demonstrated in MIT's ShyBot experiment[221] where a robot equipped with solar panels was set loose in California with the mandate that it was to avoid people.[222] ShyBot subsequently went missing for a year.[223] While this may not demonstrate intelligence, it demonstrates an element of survivability, as described by Warwick's definition of intelligence.[224] ShyBot may even have completely satisfied his definition of intelligence.

Autopoiesis can theoretically exist in both hardware and software, although autopoietic software is far more demonstrable than autopoietic hardware. Autopoiesis on its own is not sufficient for a computer hardware or software to assume legal culpability however, in the same way that a person cannot be guilty of a crime for simply breathing.[225] The introduction of intelligence alongside

---

[221]    Rosalind    W.    Picard,    'ShyBot'    (MIT,    2007) <https://www.media.mit.edu/projects/shybot/overview/>    accessed    14 October 2018

[222] Jori Finkel, 'Things Go Awry at 'Desert X,' as Shy Bot Disappears' (New York Times,           17th           March           2017) <https://www.nytimes.com/2017/03/17/arts/design/desert-x-show-things-go-awry-shy-bot-disappears.html> accessed 14 October 2018

[223] Jori Finkel, 'After a year-long journey in the California desert, Desert X's art rover   Shybot   is   found'   (The   Art   Newspaper,   25th   July   2018) <https://www.theartnewspaper.com/news/desert-x-rover-shybot-is-found-in-the-california-desert> accessed 14 October 2018

[224] Warwick (n 105)

[225] International Criminal Court Act 2001 S.50

autopoiesis creates new problems in law which will need to be addressed by the courts eventually,[226] such as where a programmer could potentially create a digital imitation of a totipotent stem cell[227] or an autopoietic computer virus that formed a neural network.[228]

## 2. Understanding the Problem

The problem that the law faces currently, with regards to developments in artificial intelligence, has multiple facets.[229] Combining autopoiesis with learning allows for what could be described as a computer organism,[230] not only capable of intelligent action but also

[226] *Privacy International v Secretary of State for Foreign and Commonwealth Affairs, Secretary of State for the Home Department, Government Communications Headquarters, Security Service, Secret Intelligence Service* [2018] 4 All ER 275, 90; see also Pratap Devarapalli, 'Machine learning to machine owning: redefining the copyright ownership from the perspective of Australian, US, UK and EU law' [2018] 40(11) European Interlectual Property Review 722

[227] Daniel R Marshak, David Gottlieb and Richard L Gardner, *Stem Cell Biology* (Cold Spring Harbour Laboratory Press 2000) 426; see also Szilvassy SJ and others, 'Quantitative assay for totipotent reconstituting hematopoietic stem cells by a competitive repopulation strategy.' [1990] 87 Proc Natl Acad Sci 8736

[228] Maturana (n 1); see also Freitas (n 218); Chang (n 216); CISCO (n 219); Matthew Griffin, 'IBM injected a virus into a neural net to create an undetectable cyberweapon' (Fanatical Futurist, 27th August 2018) <https://www.fanaticalfuturist.com/2018/08/ibm-created-an-undetectable-cyberweapon-by-injecting-viruses-into-neural-nets/ > accessed 06 April 2019

[229] Müller (n 82)

[230] George Dvorsky, 'Breakthrough: The First Complete Computer Model of a Living Organism' (Gizmodo Biology, 23rd July 2012) <https://io9.gizmodo.com/breakthrough-the-first-complete-computer-model-of-a-li-5928218> accessed 06 April 2019

of self-maintenance and potentially growth. ANN's and other forms of AI are already in use or currently being designed for use in Medicine,[231] Stock Trading,[232] Textiles,[233] Games,[234] Military Environments,[235] Automated Driving,[236] and even Law,[237] to name a few of the largest industries currently utilising the technology. These industries have their own unique legal issues, from misdiagnosis through to road traffic accidents.

The focus of this research will be on those issues which could give rise to a case of gross negligence manslaughter.[238] The contemporary legal issues such as

---

[231] Arvin Agah, *Medical Applications of Artificial Intelligence* (1st edn, CRC Press 6th November 2013); see also Diego Galar Pascual, *Artificial Intelligence Tools: Decision Support Systems in Condition Monitoring and Diagnosis* (1st edn, CRC Press 22nd April 2015); Todd A Kuiken, Aimee E Schultz Feuser and Ann K Barlow, *Targeted Muscle Reinnervation: A Neural Interface for Artificial Limbs* (1st edn, CRC Press 23rd July 2013)

[232] Stephen Slade, *Artificial Intelligence Applications on Wall Street* (1st edn, Routledge 30th November 2017)

[233] Tasnim N Shaikh and Sweety A Agrawal, *Engineering Cotton Yarns with Artificial Neural Networking (ANN)* (1st edn, WPI Publishing 5th December 2017)

[234] Millington (n 130)

[235] Jens Stoltenberg, 'The Three Ages of NATO: An Evolving Alliance' (NATO, 23rd September 2016) <https://www.nato.int/cps/en/natohq/opinions_135317.htm?selectedLocale=en> accessed 01 March 2018

[236] Lipson (n 82)

[237] Bernard Marr, 'How AI and Machine Learning are transforming Law Firms and the Legal Sector' (Forbes, 23rd May 2018) <https://www.forbes.com/sites/bernardmarr/2018/05/23/how-ai-and-machine-learning-are-transforming-law-firms-and-the-legal-sector/> accessed 06 July 2018

whether or not a person can own intellectual property produced by an AI,[239] or the applications that learning algorithms have in fraud detection,[240] will not be considered except to support a conclusion on how the courts could better address problems arising from AI and its potential involvement in cases of GNM. The benefits of AI in other areas[241] also add weight to the argument against a complete ban on development, an important consideration.[242]

The AEVA[243] creates provisions for certain aspects of the Automated Vehicle (AV) industry.[244] The AV industry

---

[238] *Adomako* (n 6)

[239] Burkhard Schafer, 'The future of IP law in an age of artificial intelligence.' [2016] 13(3) Scripted 283; see also Sanjana Kapila, 'A glimpse into the future.' [2018] 278 Managing Intellectual Property 30; Katharine Stephens and Tony Bond, 'Artificial intelligence: navigating the IP challenges' [2018] 29(6) PLC Magazine 39

[240] *Wang Laboratories Inc.'s Application* [1991] RPC 463, 465-466; see also Matt Byrne, 'Fraud watchdog enters brave new world of AI innovation.' [2018] Oct Lawyer 8; Scott Zoldi, 'Tin ears - machine learning set against social engineering.' [2018] Oct/Nov Fraud intelligence 21; Joy Macknight, 'The new age of AI fraud detection.' [2017] Oct Banker 40

[241] Agah (n 231); see also Pascual (n 231); Kuiken (n 231); Shaikh (n 233); Marr (n 237)

[242] Ian Sample, 'Thousands of leading AI researchers sign pledge against killer robots' (Guardian, 18th July 2018) <https://www.theguardian.com/science/2018/jul/18/thousands-of-scientists-pledge-not-to-help-build-killer-ai-robots> accessed 06 April 2019; see also Sulleyman (n 71); Cellan-Jones (n 71)

[243] AEVA (n 72)

[244] Waymo, 'Waymo' (Waymo, 5th December 2018) <https://waymo.com/> accessed 06 April 2019

alongside the games industry,[245] medicine industry[246] and military applications[247] still present many open legal issues despite the current legislation. The recent case in Arizona in which an AV hit and killed a pedestrian[248] only illustrates the importance of anticipating and regulating these industries far in advance of the problems occurring.[249] The broader problems that are currently being faced in terms of the development and deployment of AI were discussed by key scientists within Google's DeepMind laboratory, in the paper 'Concrete Problems in AI Safety' (CPAIS).[250]

CPAIS defines an accident as where the creator of the program has one goal or objective and the ANN[251] or AI[252] does something unexpected or harmful.[253] In the Arizona case,[254] the automated vehicle was equipped with

---

[245] Millington (n 130)

[246] Agah (n 231); see also Pascual (n 231); Kuiken (n 231)

[247] Stoltenberg (n 235)

[248] Sam Levin, 'Uber crash shows 'catastrophic failure' of self-driving technology, experts say' (The Guardian, 22nd March 2018) <https://www.theguardian.com/technology/2018/mar/22/self-driving-car-uber-death-woman-failure-fatal-crash-arizona> accessed 03 December 2018

[249] Müller (n 82); see also ibid; Sample (n 242)

[250] Amodei (n 76)

[251] Konar (n 118)

[252] Techopedia Staff, 'What is the difference between artificial intelligence and neural networks?' (Technopedia, 2nd June 2017) <https://www.techopedia.com/2/27888/programming/what-is-the-difference-between-artificial-intelligence-and-neural-networks> accessed 11 April 2019

[253] Amodei (n 76) 2

[254] Levin (n 248)

"lidar"[255] sensors designed to avoid collisions, and yet it collided with a pedestrian. In this instance the fault was probably not a catastrophic systems failure[256] but, in future incidents, this result could occur for a number of other reasons such as reward hacking or a lack of robustness to distributional shift (LRDS).[257] These are problems that could occur with people, although potentially less often.

The mention of the possibility of accidents,[258] many of which have been described in CPAIS, adds weight to the argument that although specific outcomes may not be precisely predicted, harm is a foreseeable result of negligent AI development. Crucially, this does not mean that every accident which occurs is the result of negligent AI development, but it places limitations on the counter argument that any sufficiently intelligent machine would have such free will and complexity as to be unpredictable[259] for the purpose of satisfying the foreseeability element.[260]

---

[255] NOAA, 'What is LIDAR?' (National Oceanic and Atmospheric Administration, 25th May 2018) <https://oceanservice.noaa.gov/facts/lidar.html> accessed 11 April 2019

[256] Hannah Summers, 'Uber suspends fleet of self-driving cars following Arizona crash' (The Guardian, 26th March 2017) <https://www.theguardian.com/technology/2017/mar/26/uber-suspends-self-driving-cars-arizona-crash-volvo-suv> accessed 13 April 2019

[257] Amodei (n 76) 3

[258] ibid 2

[259] Lehman (n 34)

[260] *Adomako* (n 6)

What this demonstrates, ultimately, is that scientists currently are able to anticipate problems.

In the case of LRDS[261] an example might be an automated vehicle which has been trained to get from point A to point B[262] as quickly as possible whilst adhering to the highway code[263] and all applicable laws,[264] in a simulated environment without people present it may perform this task exceptionally,[265] and then when people are introduced in a real world situation the program would not have learned to avoid them. This kind of LRDS issue could apply to any unanticipated problem, from potholes[266] through to poor weather[267] or off-road conditions[268] and has the potential to occur with humans too.

---

[261] Amodei (n 76) 3

[262] Wayve, 'Learning to drive in a day.' (Wayve Research, 28th June 2018) <https://wayve.ai/blog/learning-to-drive-in-a-day-with-reinforcement-learning> accessed 13 April 2019

[263] GOV.UK, 'The Highway Code' (GOV.UK, 1st October 2015) <https://www.gov.uk/guidance/the-highway-code> accessed 22 December 2018

[264] Road Traffic Act 1988

[265] Emilio García-Roselló and Others, 'Visual NNet: An Educational ANN's Simulation Environment Reusing Matlab Neural Networks Toolbox' (2011) 10 Informatics in Education 2, 225

[266] Helen Coffey, 'UK Drivers spend £4bn repairing car damage caused by potholes each year' (The Independent, 9th April 2019) <https://www.independent.co.uk/travel/news-and-advice/potholes-spend-uk-drivers-cost-damaged-roads-a8861376.html> accessed 13 April 2019

[267] Gov.uk (n 260) 226-237

[268] *Brown v Paterson* [2010] EWCA Civ 184, 3

LRDS could apply to a human doctor that has never operated on a person who is morbidly obese.[269] It is important to consider that in this kind of scenario where human life is at risk,[270] the foreseeable uncertainty in the machine's response could be a substitution for actual foreseeability of a specific response where the latter exceeds the requirements for negligence to be established.[271] It is also much easier to apply a punishment to a person than to a machine,[272] and this stems from the origins of legal punishment, some suggest as far back as the dawn of human society.[273]

Applying the *Adomako*[274] test to the AV scenario, the proximity element of the test could be satisfied easily, between the passengers and the victim, with *Bourhill*.[275] The problem then arises of proximity[276] between the victim

---

[269] Sharmeen Lotia and Mark C Bellamy, 'Anaesthesia and morbid obesity' [2008] 8(5) Continuing Education in Anaesthesia Critical Care & Pain 151

[270] Claire Brock, 'Risk, Responsibility and Surgery in the 1890s and Early 1900s' [2013] 57(3) Med Hist 317

[271] Rowley (n 27), 29

[272] Emerging Technology, 'When an AI finally kills someone, who will be responsible?' (MIT Technology Review, 12th March 2018) <https://www.technologyreview.com/s/610459/when-an-ai-finally-kills-someone-who-will-be-responsible/> accessed 14 April 2019

[273] Allen E Buchanan, *The Evolution of Moral Progress: A Biocultural Theory* (Oxford University Press 2018) 125; see also Gwen Robinson and Fergus McNeill, *Community Punishment: European perspectives* (Routledge 2015) 209-219; Peter Hammerstein, *Genetic and Cultural Evolution of Cooperation* (MIT Press 2003) 457-458

[274] *Adomako* (n 6)

[275] *Bourhill* (n 11) 96

and the programmers. It would be sensible in this instance to perhaps view the programmer of the AV software as the 'driver by proxy', in which case the decision is whether the driver of a car has sufficient proximity to other road users,[277] it is also established that the experience level of a road user should not stop a duty of care[278] from being owed.[279]

*Nettleship*[280] establishes that a learner driver must be held to the same standard as any other driver and this principle could be applied to a learning algorithm[281] where that algorithm is given charge of a vehicle or other sufficiently complex or potentially dangerous process.[282] This precedent could also be taken to imply that the learner is not the responsibility of the teacher however,[283] in the sense that if a learner is being held to the same driving standard as a qualified driver then perhaps the AV should be held to the same standard independently from the programmer and his instruction.[284]

---

[276] ibid

[277] *Nettleship v Weston* [1971] 2 QB 691, 2

[278] *Adomako* (n 6)

[279] *Nettleship* (n 274)

[280] ibid

[281] Nanning Zheng and Jianru Xue, *Statistical Learning and Pattern Analysis for Image and Video Processing* (Springer Science & Business Media, 2009) 171

[282] Health and Safety Executive, 'Identify the hazards' (Health and Safety Executive, 8th April 2019) <http://www.hse.gov.uk/risk/identify-the-hazards.htm> accessed 15 April 2019

[283] *Pook v Rossall School* [2018] EWHC 522 (QB), 25

[284] Appendix C

The application of *Nettleship*[285] to imply a responsibility on the programmer or the program would depend on the degree of separation between the two.[286] If the program was deemed to be a clear extension of the programmer's intent then *Nettleship*[287] would imply the same responsibility for the programmer as any other road user. Otherwise, if the programs actions and intent were separable from the programmer then the precedent could imply that the program should be held to the same standard as any other road user.[288] The latter of which could absolve the programmer of responsibility to some degree, possibly entirely.[289]

The principle of *volenti non fit injuria*[290] states that a person placing themselves in a risky situation cannot sue for damages resulting from the assumed risks, if a reasonable person would have foreseen the damage done.[291] While this principle, as a principle in tort law, would not impact the verdict in a case of GNM, it could play an important role in sentencing as a potential mitigating factor.[292]

---

[285] *Nettleship* (n 274)

[286] *Wembridge v Winter* [2013] EWHC 2331 (QB), 218; see also *R v Gurphal Singh* [1999] Crim LR 582

[287] *Nettleship* (n 274)

[288] Technology (n 269)

[289] cf Daniel Greenberg, 'Joint enterprise', Insight (16 August 2018) <Westlaw> accessed 18 April 2019

[290] Helen Bain, 'Raybould v T&N Gilmartin (Contractors) Ltd: when can the defence of volenti non fit injuria apply?' [2019] 145 Civil Practice Bulletin, 3

[291] *McLaughlin v Morrison* [2014] SLT 111, 29

Where a person has knowingly exposed themselves to the risk of grossly negligent software, by entering a situation where the computer is in control, the defendant may be partially absolved of blame.

The foreseeability need not be actual foreseeability,[293] so in this example the programmers would not need to actually foresee that their actions would result in a specific person's death, it would only need to be foreseeable that poor computer code could result in harm when that code was given control of a heavy motorised vehicle.[294] This presents the problem that, arguably, harm can be foreseen to some extent when responsibility is given to any sufficiently intelligent[295] and autonomous individual. It is a foreseeable possibility that a human driver may crash a car,[296] the DVLA would not be guilty of GNM.

The reason that the DVLA would not be held responsible is down to the assumption that the human

---

[292] Nick Barnard, 'Culpability and mitigation – sentencing in medical gross negligence manslaughter' (CorkerBinning, 20th January 2016) <https://www.corkerbinning.com/culpability-and-mitigation-sentencing-in-medical-gross-negligence-manslaughter/> accessed 18 April 2019

[293] *Rowley* (n 27)

[294] AEVA (n 72) S4(1)(b)

[295] James W Trent, *Inventing the Feeble Mind: A History of Intellectual Disability in the United States* (Oxford University Press 2017) 263-266

[296] Lydia Jackson and Richard Cracknell, 'Road accident casualties in Britain and the world' (2018) Commons Briefing Papers CBP-7615 <https://researchbriefings.parliament.uk/ResearchBriefing/Summary/CBP-7615#fullreport> accessed 18 April 2019

driver is acting independently,[297] the licence and training provided to the driver are secondary to their own logic and reasoning skills.[298] In essence a human being has common sense,[299] therefore it would not be reasonable to hold the DVLA responsible for a person's actions in most cases. Where the training provided to the driver was not acceptable then the DVLA should not licence the person,[300] this is assessed through various tests.[301] A machine which has common sense should perhaps be assessed similarly.

The fair, just and reasonable element[302] of the negligence would need to be subjective[303] based on the facts of any given case. If the programmer could prove that the program itself had learned,[304] then the proximity element[305] here may not be satisfied, this could be defined

---

[297] *Nettleship* (n 274)

[298] RAC, 'Drivers urged to use common sense' (Press Association, 14th January 2010) <https://www.rac.co.uk/drive/news/motoring-news/Drivers-urged-to-use-common-sense/> accessed 19 April 2019; see also Government of South Australia, 'The Driver's Handbook: Care, Courtesy, Common Sense' (Government of South Australia: Department of Planning, Transport and Infrastructure, 25th October 2009) <http://mylicence.sa.gov.au/road-rules/the-drivers-handbook/care-courtesy> accessed 19 April 2019

[299] John McCarthy, 'Programs with Common Sense' [1968] Semantic Information Processing, 403

[300] The Motor Vehicles (Driving Licences) Regulations 1999 S17(c)

[301] ibid S17

[302] *Hill* (n 14); see also Steele (n 14)

[303] *McQuire v Western Morning News Company, Limited* [1903] 2 KB 100, 109

[304] Ethem Alpaydin, *Machine Learning: The New AI* (1st edn, MIT Press 2016); see also Ethem Alpaydin, *Introduction to Machine Learning* (3rd edn, MIT Press 2014)

as the argument that the programmer's intent had become sufficiently detached from the programs intent so as to make the substitution unreasonable. This lack of proximity between the programmer and the victim of GNM would not equate to a lack of proximity between the program and the victim or the owner and the victim.

If the court is predominantly made up of Descartes dualists,[306] then the argument would be that a computer can never have consciousness or the ability to learn because the mind is a different kind of "stuff".[307] A Chalmers[308] dualist or a monist materialist such as Democritus[309] would perhaps argue that the program itself can have consciousness, although each would differ on the reason why. These philosophical positions are mostly concerned with fundamental assessment, they focus on defining the nature of a process in its entirety, so that something may be said to have, or not have, constitution of that nature.

Philosophy should not eclipse factual assessment however, where a program was created without the ability

[305] *Bourhill* (n 11)

[306] Descartes (n 85)

[307] Samuel Guttenplan, *A Companion to the Philosophy of Mind* (Blackwell Publishers 1994) 265-268

[308] David J Chalmers, *The Conscious Mind: In Search of a Fundamental Theory* (Oxford University Press USA 1997) 123-131; see also ibid 514-519

[309] B Hergenhahn, *An Introduction to the History of Psychology* (Cengage Learning 2004) 34

to perform a task[310] and then through independent observation becomes able to perform a task,[311] the philosophy behind the name for that process is less important than the process itself. The law is concerned with the outcome,[312] the process undertaken is useful for a better assessment of the situation but the understanding of why the process has occurred is less important.[313] It is essential to understand how well the machine can now perform the task, not how it came to be able to perform it.[314]

In this case, the question of consciousness confuses the issue, to offer a legal alternative to Chalmers "hard" and "easy" problems,[315] the hard question in this case would be whether the program satisfies consciousness[316] and the easy question would be whether the program has changed in a way that could not have been foreseen. Only the easy question would need to be decided to determine a lack of foreseeability,[317] but the

---

[310] Waymo (n 244)

[311] ibid

[312] Jeremy Horder, 'Strict liability, statutory construction, and the spirit of liberty' [2002] 118(Jul) Law Quarterly Review 458

[313] Rebecca Huxley-Binns, *Criminal Law Concentrate* (Oxford University Press 2014) 20-21

[314] Turing (n 37) 433-436

[315] Jonathan Shear, *Explaining Consciousness: The Hard Problem* (MIT Press 1999) 6

[316] Pentti O Haikonen, *Consciousness and Robot Sentience* (World Scientific Publishing Co 2012) 73-78; see also Owen Holland, *Machine Consciousness* (Imprint Academic 2003)

[317] *Jessica Griffiths, Hannah Griffiths, Sophie Griffiths, (A minor by her father*

hard question still has relevance when considering solutions and further issues such as the question of causation.[318] Fault and punishment may not be applicable in situations involving intelligent machines.[319]

The programs ability to make decisions and the origin of that ability are pivotal to the entire *Adomako* test,[320] in any scenario involving a learning machine. This places an onus on the creator of any learning machine to assess the stability of the program and the risks[321] associated with the deployment, pre-emptively. From a paternalistic perspective[322] however, it may be better to enforce this concept legally; instead of allowing companies and individuals to enforce their own standards.[323] Defining the standard of care to be enforced creates many more issues,

---

*and Litigation Friend Jeremy Griffiths) v The Chief Constable of the Suffolk Police, Norfolk and Suffolk NHS Foundation Trust* [2018] EWHC 2538 (QB), 203; see also *Andrew Winterton v Regina* [2018] EWCA Crim 2435, 4; *Polemis v Furness Withy & Co* [1921] 3 K.B. 560, 563; *Overseas Tankship (U.K.) Ltd v Morts Dock & Engineering Co Ltd (the Wagon Mound)* [1961] A.C. 388; Ian Meikle, 'Foreseeability', Insight (10 July 2018) <Westlaw> accessed 20 April 2019

[318] *R v Mohammed Khalique Zaman* [2017] EWCA Crim 1783, 49

[319] Technology (n 269)

[320] *Adomako* (n 6)

[321] Health (n 279)

[322] Russ Shafer-Landau, 'Liberalism and paternalism' [2005] 11(3) Legal Theory 169

[323] Joseph Lee, 'Shareholders' derivative claims under the Companies Act 2006: market mechanism or asymmetric paternalism?' [2007] 18(11) International Company and Commercial Law Review 378

but could save time, money and possibly people's lives, in future.

Negligence itself spans across many areas but becomes particularly relevant within professional environments[324] where an individual is expected to operate on a level above that of an ordinary person.[325] The classic example of elevated expectation is within medical negligence, where a doctor is expected to respond differently to a layman in certain instances.[326] Expert systems[327] have been in use within medical environments for many years,[328] but many areas of medicine are now making use of other types of AI such as ANNs which have now been utilised for the purpose of cancer diagnosis.[329] This creates the possibility of AI misdiagnosis.

---

[324] *Hadiza Bawa-Garba v The General Medical Council v The British Medical Association, The Professional Standards Authority for Health and Social Care, The British Association of Physicians of Indian Origin* [2018] EWCA Civ 1879, 12; see also *North West Anglia NHS Foundation Trust v Dr Andrew Gregg* [2019] EWCA Civ 387, 4; *Regina (Birks) v Commissioner of Police of the Metropolis and another (No 2)* [2018] ICR 1400, 48

[325] Nadia N Sawicki, 'Judging Doctors: The Person and the Professional' [2011] 10(13) AMA Journal of Ethics 718

[326] ibid

[327] The Export of Goods (Control) Order 1989 IL1566(b)(5)(ii); see also *Wang* (n 240); Abdul Paliwala, 'Rediscovering artificial intelligence and law: an adequate jurisprudence?' [2016] 30(3) International Review of Law Computers and Technology 107

[328] *BSkyB Limited, Sky Subscribers Services Limited v HP Enterprise Services UK Limited (formerly Electronic Data Systems Limited), Electronic Data systems LLC (Formerly Electronic Data Systems Corporation)* [2010] EWHC 86 (TCC), 274

In a military environment, it could be much more difficult to determine whether a program has acted as intended.[330] Where a Predator drone[331] has been tasked with autonomously responding to threat[332] by preserving itself and eliminating enemy combatants[333] and where that drone is responding to instructions from an ANN[334] acting as a Reconnaissance-Strike-Network[335] controller, it may be difficult to separate where the drone has neutralized a combatant because the combatant posed a threat to the drone, to personnel on the ground or simply because the combatant had red hair. Therefore, the standard of care required should perhaps differ between industries.

This is the issue where all targets within the training simulation may have had a common feature which was negligently overlooked by the programmer. A programmer tasked with producing an ANN could be responsible for driving thousands of people to work[336] or launching military

[329] RNG Naguib and GV Sherbet, *Artificial Neural Networks in Cancer Diagnosis, Prognosis, and Patient Management* (1st edn, CRC Press 2001)

[330] Amodei (n 76) 7-11

[331] Paul Scharre, *Robotics on the Battlefield – Part 1: Range, Persistence and Daring* (Center for a New American Security, 2014) 140-151

[332] Ministry of Defence, A Soldier's Guide to the Law of Armed Conflict (2005) Document Number AC71130 <https://assets.publishing.service.gov.uk/government/uploads/system/uploads/attachment_data/file/619906/2017-04714.pdf> accessed 10 November 2018

[333] MOD (n 332) [3.1]-[3.3]

[334] Konar (n 118)

[335] Scharre (n 328) 81-108

offensives subject to the law of armed conflict (LOAC),[337] thus a much higher standard of care is required because while an error made by one driver may have an impact on many lives, an error mirrored by thousands of drivers or thousands of doctors[338] has the potential to impact an exponentially larger number of lives.

Learning machines which have been deployed into society[339] can be broadly placed into two categories; static and dynamic. Dynamic learning machines (DLM) would continue to learn following deployment,[340] whereas static learning machines (SLM) would only learn prior to their deployment.[341] The former would have increased potential for success within new environments,[342] but the latter

---

[336] Shehab Khan, 'Self-driving taxis to be launched in London by 2021, Addison Lee says' (The Independent, 22nd October 2018) <https://www.independent.co.uk/news/uk/home-news/self-driving-taxis-london-addison-lee-ride-sharing-technology-a8595381.html> accessed 20 April 2019; see also Waymo (n 244)

[337] MoD (n 329)

[338] A Shademan and others, 'Supervised autonomous robotic soft tissue surgery' [2016] 8(337) Sci Transl Med 337

[339] Christian Szegedy and others, 'Going Deeper with Convolutions' [2014] Google Inc <https://arxiv.org/pdf/1409.4842.pdf> accessed 20 April 2019

[340] Alexander Mordvintsev, 'DeepDream - a code example for visualizing Neural Networks' (Google AI Blog, 1st July 2015) <https://ai.googleblog.com/2015/07/deepdream-code-example-for-visualizing.html> accessed 20 April 2019; see also Waymo (n 244); ibid

[341] cf Stackify, 'Dev Leaders Compare Continuous Delivery vs. Continuous Deployment vs. Continuous Integration' (Stackify, 25th July 2017) <https://stackify.com/continuous-delivery-vs-continuous-deployment-vs-continuous-integration/> accessed 20 April 2019

[342] Daniel Graupe, *Principles of Artificial Neural Networks* (World Scientific

would potentially be much easier to anticipate. The law would struggle to place the responsibility for a DLM on the programmer, because the state the machine was in upon deployment could have changed substantially.[343] Similarly, a parent may not be held responsible for their adult children.[344]

In the first instance, the simplest solution is to hold the creator of the program responsible for their creation,[345] but this may not be considered a fair solution.[346] If parents were held accountable for every decision that their children made in life, this could result in parents going to prison for a murder committed by their forty-year-old child.[347] This raises the question of whether AI should have an age of majority,[348] where it is considered to have learned enough,[349] however this would be nearly impossible to state in years

2007) 2

[343] Waymo (n 244)

[344] Children and Young Persons Act 1933 S50; see also Hawkins Spizman Fortas, 'Are Parents Responsible for Children's Crimes?' (Hawkins Spizman Fortas, 20th December 2018) <https://www.hsflawfirm.com/are-parents-responsible-for-childrens-crimes/> accessed 20 April 2019

[345] Copyright, Designs and Patents Act 1988 S9(1)

[346] *Hill* (n 14); see also Steele (n 14)

[347] *James Douglas Ferguson v Her Majesty's Advocate* [2014] HCJAC 19, 43

[348] TE James, 'The Age of Majority' (1960) 4(1) American Journal of Legal History 22

[349] Sharyn Neuwirth, *Learning Disabilities* (Diane Publishing 1993) 10-14; see also Organisation for Economic Coordination and Development, *Understanding the Brain: The Birth of a Learning Science* (OECD 2007) 110

due to the independent variables involved in each machine's learning process.[350]

Once autopoietic computer systems are considered,[351] the problem relates more closely to whether or not great grandparents should be held responsible for their grandchildren. DLMs that produce other DLMs[352] with the goal of creating a slightly better version each time can develop not just a difference between the programmer's intention and its own, but could also develop a new code layout which may not be coherent to the original programmer.[353] Autopoiesis would allow code to evolve, making it both self-sufficient and reproductive.[354] It is easier to object mathematically[355] or due to the informality of behaviour[356] whilst a system is understood.[357]

---

[350] Pablo Rudomin and others, *Neuroscience: From Neural Networks to Artificial Intelligence: Proceedings of a U.S.-Mexico Seminar held in the city of Xalapa in the state of Veracruz on December 9–11, 1991* (Springer Science & Business Media 2012) 338

[351] Maturana (n 1); see also Dvorsky (n 230); Freitas (n 218); Chang (n 216); CISCO (n 219); Griffin (n 228)

[352] Chang (n 216)

[353] Shelby Rogers, 'Google's AI Now Creates Code Better Than its Creators' (Interesting Engineering, 18th October 2017) <https://interestingengineering.com/googles-ai-now-creates-code-better-than-its-creators> accessed 20 April 2019

[354] Maturana (n 1); see also Dvorsky (n 230); Freitas (n 218); Chang (n 216); CISCO (n 219); Griffin (n 228)

[355] Turing (n 37) 444-445; see also Piccinini (n 163); Copeland (n 163)

[356] Turing (n 37) 452

[357] Lars Skyttner, *General Systems Theory: Problems, Perspectives, Practice* (World Scientific 2005) 3-48

The age of criminal responsibility for humans is currently ten years old in the UK,[358] and this age could be described as the age at which the courts allow a 'defence of separation' where a child can be deemed to have learned enough to be responsible for their own actions. A computers rate of learning would depend on many things, including the complexity of its code,[359] its processing power[360] and the amount of training data[361] it was provided with. These variables and others could be used to create a universal measurement for a computer's learning speed, which would allow comparisons.[362]

In the second instance, if neither programmers nor their creations are held accountable for death caused by the action or inaction of the computer then a situation could

---

[358] CYPA (n 341); see also Hawkins (n 341)

[359] June Jamrich Parsons, *New Perspectives Computer Concepts 2016 Enhanced, Comprehensive* (Cengage Learning 2016) 765; see also Fernando Ferri, *Visual Languages for Interactive Computing: Definitions and Formalizations* (Idea Group Inc (IGI) 2008) 15; Dana H Ballard, *Brain Computation as Hierarchical Abstraction* (MIT Press 2015) 15

[360] Appendix A

[361] Věra Kůrková and others, *Artificial Neural Networks and Machine Learning – ICANN 2018: 27th International Conference on Artificial Neural Networks, Rhodes, Greece, October 4-7, 2018, Proceedings, Part 3* (Springer 2018) 256; see also James Kwok, Liqing Zhang and Bao-Liang Lu, *Advances in Neural Networks -- ISNN 2010: 7th International Symposium on Neural Networks, ISNN 2010, Shanghai, China, June 6-9, 2010, Proceedings* (Springer Science & Business Media, 20 May 2010) 347; Stephen W Ellacott, John C Mason and Iain J Anderson, *Mathematics of Neural Networks: Models, Algorithms and Applications* (Springer Science & Business Media 1997) 192

[362] Appendix A

arise where a computer could kill without consequence,[363] potentially even giving rise to situations where lethal computer code[364] is used intentionally by someone other than the programmer to cause death. There would need to be a system in place to stop this kind of abuse, even in a broad form such as with the CMA.[365] This may be difficult for the public to accept due to the blanket nature of broad legislation.[366]

In the final instance, where the computer is held accountable for its own actions, there exists the problem of punishment,[367] prevention,[368] and control.[369] It is difficult to apply the law to something which has been granted legal

---

[363] David J Gunkel, *The Machine Question: Critical Perspectives on AI, Robots, and Ethics* (MIT Press 2012) 16

[364] Kesler (n 80); see also Zetter (n 80); Farwell (n 80)

[365] CMA (n 46)

[366] Shepherd and Wedderburn LLP, 'Changes to the Computer Misuse Act' (Lexology, 10th December 2008) <https://www.lexology.com/library/detail.aspx?g=84d37161-052e-4c40-b97d-408321679364> accessed 23 April 2019; see also Ahmad Nehaluddin, 'Hackers' criminal behaviour and laws related to hacking' [2009] 15(7) Computer and Telecommunications Law Review 159

[367] Buchanan (n 270); see also Robinson (n 270); Hammerstein (n 270); Technology (n 269)

[368] Henrique Carvalho, *The Preventive Turn in Criminal Law* (Oxford university Press 2017) 13-16; see also Andrew Ashworth, Lucia Zedner and Patrick Tomlin, *Prevention and the Limits of the Criminal Law* (Oxford university Press 2013); Richard S Gruner, *Corporate Criminal Liability and Prevention* (Law Journal Press 2004) §2.06

[369] Qi Chen, *Governance, Social Control and Legal Reform in China: Community Sanctions and Measures* (Springer 2018) 50; see also Larry Siegel, *Essentials of Criminal Justice* (Cengage Learning 2008) 35-36

personhood[370] but which may not have the same fear of punishment that humans would have. Likewise it is also very difficult to exert control over something that can exist in data form in multiple places at one time.[371] Prevention is therefore the logical solution to the broader problem. This is difficult to implement, especially when considering the lack of extensive expertise currently available.[372]

---

[370] Louise Amoore, 'Risk before justice: when the law contests its own suspension' [2008] 21(4) Leiden Journal of International Law 847, 861; see also Ford (n 94)

[371] David A Patterson and John L Hennessy, *Computer Organization and Design: The Hardware/Software Interface* (Morgan Kaufmann 2008) 602; see also Howard Gordon, 'The Multivendor Muddle: Heterogeneous local-area networks face proprietary road blocks.' [1986] 35(3) Network World 43, 44

[372] Michaela Ross, 'Tech-Savvy Attorneys in Heavy Demand Amid Emerging Tech' (Bloomberg Law, 22nd February 2018) <https://www.bna.com/techsavvy-attorneys-heavy-n57982089186/> accessed 25 April 2019; see also James Warrington, 'Hacker stereotypes exacerbate UK's cyber security skills shortage, warns NCSC' (City AM, 11th February 2019) <http://www.cityam.com/273066/computer-geek-stereotypes-causing-cyber-security-skills> accessed 25 April 2019

## 3. Forming a Solution

If fault could not be applied to situations involving death because a learning machine was involved, this could create a strong opposition to the use of technology in many industries.[373] Where a learning machine cannot be punished for its actions, the incentive for it to perform better must be built on something else,[374] this creates a divide between law and technology. A fundamental principle behind punishment in criminal law is as a preventative measure within society,[375] but if a section of society is 'immune'[376] then it becomes difficult to justify the punishment of the remainder. Hypocrisy becomes a core issue.[377]

The broadness of legislation related to technology has been criticised in the past, especially in the case of the

---

[373] Theo Dimitrakos and others, *Formal Aspects in Security and Trust: Third International Workshop, FAST 2005, Newcastle upon Tyne, UK, July 18-19, 2005, Revised Selected Papers* (Springer 2006) 187; see also David Salomon, *Foundations of Computer Security* (Springer Science & Business Media 2006) 261; Stair Baldauf, *Instructor Edition: Succeeding with Technology 2005 Update* (Course Technology 2005) 452

[374] Antonio Gulli and Sujit Pal, *Deep Learning with Keras* (Packt Publishing Ltd 2017) 265-288; see also Richard S Sutton and Andrew G Barto, *Reinforcement Learning: An Introduction* (MIT Press 2018)

[375] Carvalho (n 365); see also Ashworth (n 365); Gruner (n 365)

[376] Diplomatic Privileges Act 1964

[377] Ashley Deeks, 'Diplomatic immunity protects even Erdogan's thugs. We have to live with that.' (The Washington Post, 18th May 2017) <https://www.washingtonpost.com/posteverything/wp/2017/05/18/diplomatic-immunity-protects-all-officials-even-erdogans-thugs-thats-good/?noredirect=on&utm_term=.9fd8c4d89e82> accessed 26 April 2019

CMA.[378] The core issue with creating a response to this problem is that legislation is produced at a much slower rate in comparison to technology.[379] The easiest way to address this problem is to create all-encompassing legislation which does not need to be amended often.[380] There are however a number of other, potentially better, approaches that could be considered when examining the problem of adaptive software or hardware.[381] This is based on the assumption that paternalism is necessary for public safety.[382]

Prevention is the first goal of most legislation,[383] and control is a key element of this.[384] There are many actors within these potential scenarios on which control could be asserted as a preventative measure. The

---

[378] Ian Lloyd, *Information Technology Law* (Oxford University Press 2017) 218; see also Shepherd (n 363)

[379] Vyara Apostolova, 'Acts and Statutory Instruments: the volume of UK legislation 1950 to 2016' (2017) Commons Briefing Papers CBP-7438 <https://researchbriefings.parliament.uk/ResearchBriefing/Summary/CBP-7438#fullreport> accessed 27 April 2019; see also Moore (n 68)

[380] Parliament, 'What is Secondary Legislation?' (Parliament.gov.uk, 21st July 2018) <https://www.parliament.uk/about/how/laws/secondary-legislation/> accessed 27 April 2019

[381] Michael Spencer, 'Artificial Intelligence Regulation May Be Impossible' (Forbes, 2nd March 2019) <https://www.forbes.com/sites/cognitiveworld/2019/03/02/artificial-intelligence-regulation-will-be-impossible/#42210a9011ed> accessed 27 April 2019

[382] Shafer-Landau (n 319)

[383] Carvalho (n 365); see also Ashworth (n 365); Gruner (n 365)

[384] Chen (n 366); see also Siegel (n 366)

legislature could target their response at programmers,[385] computers,[386] consumers,[387] manufacturers[388] or a combination thereof, and the orientation of the response in relation to these actors will heavily impact the effectiveness of the response. It will also be necessary to discuss the subject of the legislation alongside the actors, as legislation could be applied to software,[389] hardware,[390] neither or both, with various differences in the outcomes.

Taking a preventative approach from the top down, software could be controlled by legislating on programmers.[391] Programmers are the origin of potentially dangerous code and therefore legislation on their development, use and deployment of such code could have a broad impact on the root of any potential problems.

---

[385] James Vincent, 'Tencent says there are only 300,000 AI engineers worldwide, but millions are needed' (The Verge, 5th December 2017) <https://www.theverge.com/2017/12/5/16737224/global-ai-talent-shortfall-tencent-report> accessed 27 April 2019

[386] Massimiliano Versace, 'Does Artificial Intelligence Require Specialized Processors?' (The New Stack, 20th October 2017) <https://thenewstack.io/ai-hardware-software-dilemma/> accessed 27 April 2019

[387] Cal Jeffrey, 'Machine-learning algorithm beats 20 lawyers in NDA legal analysis' (TechSpot, 31st October 2018) <https://www.techspot.com/news/77189-machine-learning-algorithm-beats-20-lawyers-nda-legal.html> accessed 27 April 2019; see also Levin (n 248)

[388] Waymo (n 244)

[389] Claire L Evans, *Broad Band: The Untold Story of the Women Who Made the Internet* (Penguin 2018) 52

[390] Ray Bradley, *Understanding Computing AS Level for AQA* (Nelson Thornes 2004) 19

[391] CMA (n 46) S1

The number of programmers is also significantly smaller than the number of consumers and computers,[392] although possibly larger than the number of manufacturers,[393] which in turn makes control much easier to assert in the form of licencing,[394] registration[395] and monitoring.[396] These forms of control are also dynamic, but more costly to enforce.[397]

On the other hand placing restrictions on programmers could have a drastic effect on the speed of development,[398] adding years to the development of new and potentially lifesaving technology.[399] Legislation with a similar purpose but instead targeting manufacturers would potentially keep development speeds unharmed, but would have an impact on deployment speeds,[400] however the

---

[392] Vincent (n 382)

[393] Jeff Dunn, 'Here are the companies that sell the most PCs worldwide' (Business Insider, 14th April 2017) <https://www.businessinsider.com/top-pc-companies-sales-idc-market-share-chart-2017-4?r=US&IR=T> accessed 27 April 2019

[394] cf Private Security Industry Act 2001 S3; see also cf Licensing Act 2003

[395] cf Companies Act 2006 S14

[396] cf SOA (n 133) S80

[397] Alon Harel and Keith N Hylton, *Research Handbook on the Economics of Criminal Law* (Edward Elgar Publishing 2012) 101; see also Carolyn Abbot, *Enforcing Pollution Control Regulation: Strengthening Sanctions and Improving Deterrence* (Bloomsbury Publishing 2009) 9

[398] Judy van Rhijn, 'Do strong IP laws stifle innovation?' (Canadian Lawyer, 3rd July 2012) <https://www.canadianlawyermag.com/author/na/do-strong-ip-laws-stifle-innovation-1662/> accessed 27 April 2019

[399] Naguib (n 326); see also Shademan (n 335)

[400] cf Chris Morris, 'Made in Britain: What does it mean for trade after Brexit?' (BBC News, 26th March 2018) <https://www.bbc.co.uk/news/uk-politics-43516496> accessed 27 April 2019

impact would possibly be offset by the value of the development.[401] Where a development is worth a lot of money, a manufacturer would potentially try harder to conform to licencing requirements than a programmer would prior to writing the code. These solutions would apply responsibility legislatively.[402]

In contrast, attempting to tackle the issue of prevention from a bottom up angle, starting with the consumers or the victims[403] has the opposite problem in that it would be very difficult to keep track of every potential misuse of software or every potential misuse of hardware.[404] A consumer-oriented prevention perspective would possibly take the form of registering offenders,[405] instigating fines[406] and other counter-incentives which are

---

[401] Louis Columbus, 'Sizing The Market Value Of Artificial Intelligence' (Forbes, 30th April 2018) <https://www.forbes.com/sites/louiscolumbus/2018/04/30/sizing-the-market-value-of-artificial-intelligence/#4e926aa4ffe9> accessed 27 April 2019

[402] Gavin Dingwall and Alisdair A Gillespie, 'Reconsidering the good Samaritan: a duty to rescue?' [2008] 39 Cambrian Law Review 26

[403] Levin (n 248)

[404] Larry Greenemeier, 'Seeking Address: Why Cyber Attacks Are So Difficult to Trace Back to Hackers' (Scientific American, 11th June 2011) <https://www.scientificamerican.com/article/tracking-cyber-hackers/> accessed 28 April 2019; see also Maggie Koerth-Baker, 'Why Global Hackers Are Nearly Impossible to Catch' (Live Science, 19th June 2008) <https://www.livescience.com/2627-global-hackers-impossible-catch.html> accessed 28 April 2019

[405] Adam Jackson, 'Sexual harm prevention orders: appropriate restrictions on internet access and the use of digital devices' [2018] 82(1) Journal of Criminal Law 11

much more punishment based.[407] Keeping track of every person who uses Facebook[408] for example, would require a government or organisation to track approximately 2.38 billion users each month, 1.15 billion active users per day.[409]

The SOA[410] currently requires individuals to become "subject to notification requirements"[411] if they commit an offence listed under schedule 3. This kind of registration[412] could be used in the context of AI development to keep track only of programmers, manufacturers and consumers that have created potentially dangerous or intelligent code.[413] The advantage of this would be that limiting the number of tracked individuals would save time and money, but this has the disadvantage of being applied reactively and not pre-emptively.[414] Reactive solutions are not ideal because the

---

[406] Criminal Justice Act 1982 S37(2); see also Daniel Greenberg, 'Strict liability (criminal)', Insight (11 January 2019) <Westlaw> accessed 28 April 2019

[407] Criminal Justice Act 2003

[408] Facebook, 'Facebook' (Facebook.Com, 28th April 2019) <https://www.facebook.com/> accessed 28 April 2019

[409] Facebook Newsroom, 'Stats' (Facebook.com, 31st March 2019) <https://newsroom.fb.com/company-info/> accessed 28 April 2019

[410] SOA (n 133)

[411] ibid S80

[412] Jackson (n 402)

[413] Kesler (n 80); see also Zetter (n 80); Farwell (n 80)

[414] Susan Donkin, *Preventing Terrorism and Controlling Risk: A Comparative Analysis of Control Orders in the UK and Australia* (Springer Science & Business Media 2013) 1-6; see also Andrew Sanders, Richard Young and Mandy Burton, *Criminal Justice* (Oxford University Press 2010) 64-65; Tamara Tulich and others, *Regulating Preventive Justice: Principle, Policy and Paradox* (Routledge

harm must have occurred or be close to occurring before they are used.[415]

Suggesting that programmers that create intelligent programs should be registered in the same way as sex offenders[416] is potentially contradictory to the public interest[417] in this instance however, because the social stigma[418] attached to such registers heavily discourages any involvement with activities that may lead to offender registration.[419] While discouraging sex offenders by enforcing registration is ideal for that type of offence, it may not be ideal in this instance due to the value that scientific advancements in artificial intelligence can have for the

---

2017); Alan M Dershowitz, *Preemption: A Knife That Cuts Both Ways* (WW Norton & Company 2006); Patrick Kelly, 'Preemptive Self-Defense, Customary International Law, and the Congolese Wars' (E-International Relations Students, 3rd September 2016) <https://www.e-ir.info/2016/09/03/preemptive-self-defense-customary-international-law-and-the-congolese-wars/> accessed 28 April 2019

[415] Gerard W Hogan and Clive Walker, *Political Violence and the Law in Ireland* (Manchester University Press 1989) 6

[416] SOA (n 133) S80

[417] Mike Feintuck and Mike Whitehouse, *'The Public Interest' in Regulation* (Oxford University Press 2004)

[418] *R (on the application of Salman Butt) v The Secretary of State for the Home Department* [2019] EWCA Civ 256, 101

[419] Chris Lobanov-Rostovsky, 'Chapter 8: Sex Offender Management Strategies' (Sex Offender Management Assessment and Planning Initiative, 24th October 2014) <https://www.smart.gov/SOMAPI/sec1/ch8_strategies.html> accessed 28 April 2019; see also ACRO, 'Managing more sex offender records than ever before' (ACRO, 5th September 2018) <https://www.acro.police.uk/acro_std.aspx?id=2288> accessed 28 April 2019

general population.[420] For this reason, it could be better to view this as a last resort.

Licencing shows much more promise than registration, for example the Private Security Industry Act[421] requires that security professionals obtain a licence before they engage in certain roles because parliament recognises that the security industry is an environment where someone without appropriate training or experience could cause harm to a member of the public.[422] Likewise, the Private Hire Vehicles (London) Act[423] requires private hire vehicle operators to hold a licence for the same reason.[424] Licencing does not have the same kind of stigma attached to it as offender registration,[425] and in many cases is used by professionals to demonstrate their competence.

---

[420] Agah (n 231); see also Pascual (n 231); Kuiken (n 231); Shaikh (n 233); Marr (n 237)

[421] Private Security Industry Act 2001 S3

[422] *Rory Davis v George Fessey, Leisure Ninety Nine Limited, West Yorkshire Security UK Limited, Ian Cox (Trading as Cox Security Services)* [2018] 4 WLUK 29; see also cf *Regina v Liam Holgate* [2019] EWCA Crim 338

[423] Private Hire Vehicles (London) Act 1998 S2

[424] *Regina v Imtiaz Hussain* [2006] EWCA Crim 1372, 3; see also Tammy Webber, 'The death of a college student who got into a car she thought was an Uber could spark a crackdown for ride-hailing safety' (Business Insider, 7th April 2019) <https://www.businessinsider.com/slaying-puts-focus-on-ride-hailing-safety-fake-drivers-2019-4?r=US&IR=T> accessed 29 April 2019

[425] *Salman* (n 415)

The commonality between these two pieces of legislation is that the professional must meet a set standard[426] before they are granted permission to apply their trade in a public environment,[427] requiring a programmer or manufacturer to obtain a licence before releasing certain types of code would allow the government to regulate[428] and review potentially dangerous software before it could be released to the general population.[429] Manufacturer licencing would place the onus on the manufacturer to ensure that the programmers code was safe, however this could have an adverse effect in requiring laymen (the manufacturers) to police the experts (the programmers).[430]

Discouraging the development of technology which could have medical benefits[431] or solve large scale social problems[432] would be counterproductive. The registration

---

[426] Security Industry Authority, 'Licence Conditions' (SIA, 1st March 2018) <https://www.sia.homeoffice.gov.uk/Pages/licensing-conditions.aspx> accessed 29 April 2019

[427] PSIA (n 418) S3(2)

[428] Security Industry Authority, 'Security Industry Authority' (SIA, 29th April 2019) <https://www.sia.homeoffice.gov.uk/Pages/home.aspx> accessed 29 April 2019; see also Financial Conduct Authority, 'Financial Conduct Authority' (FCA, 29th April 2019) <https://www.fca.org.uk/> accessed 29 April 2019

[429] Richard Murch, *The Software Development Lifecycle - A Complete Guide* (Amazon.co.uk 2012)

[430] Wilson Edward Reed, *The Politics of Community Policing: The Case of Seattle* (Routledge 2013) 96

[431] Agah (n 231); see also Pascual (n 231); Kuiken (n 231);

[432] Qiuwen Chen, *Cellular Automata and Artificial Intelligence in Ecohydraulics*

of those who commit certain offenses is very useful for keeping track of individuals that have committed certain types of crime,[433] but to suggest that the mere creation of software should amount to a crime does not tackle the problem. The problem being the deployment of dangerous software.[434] Assessing the risks associated with software could be something that the legislature takes expert advice on,[435] future legislation could then place software on a scale and mandate different actions for each.[436]

Code that learns to solve a particular problem,[437] and is then frozen at that stage of learning before being deployed, is much less likely to cause problems and would be easily regulated by requiring the programmer releasing the code to obtain a licence.[438] The problem then becomes code which is not frozen at a certain stage of learning,[439] code that is allowed or required to continue learning in a live environment has much more potential for future

*Modelling* (1st edn, CRC Press 2004)

[433] SOA (n 133) S80

[434] Kesler (n 80); see also Zetter (n 80); Farwell (n 80)

[435] Chris Skidmore, 'Adrian Smith Review:Written statement - HCWS1449' (Parliament, 26th March 2019) <https://www.parliament.uk/business/publications/written-questions-answers-statements/written-statement/Commons/2019-03-26/HCWS1449/> accessed 29 April 2019

[436] CJA (n 403)

[437] Donald J Norris, *Beginning Artificial Intelligence with the Raspberry Pi* (Apress 2017) 9-15

[438] cf PSIA (n 418); see also cf PHV(L)A (n 420)

[439] Waymo (n 244)

evolutionary issues. This kind of code would require constant supervision,[440] and this could require a separate type of licence, due to increased risks.[441]

Banning dynamic code outright would be the safest option but not the most practical and nor would it be easy to enforce, while this option can be considered it would perhaps be more sensible to review the previously mentioned criminal registration.[442] Criminal registration in an instance where intelligent or autopoietic code has caused death would not need to be enforced on the programmer but could instead be enforced via a code register.[443] This solves the fundamental issue of whether punishing the programmer is fair[444] and whether the harm was foreseeable.[445] Keeping a register of the code itself could solve this.[446]

---

[440] ibid

[441] Security Industry Authority, 'Licensable Roles' (SIA, 12th July 2018) <https://www.sia.homeoffice.gov.uk/Pages/licensing-roles.aspx> accessed 29 April 2019

[442] Jackson (n 402)

[443] Comodo, 'Anti-Malware Database' (Comodo, 21st October 2011) <https://www.comodo.com/home/internet-security/updates/vdp/database.php> accessed 29 April 2019

[444] Hill (n 14); see also Steele (n 14)

[445] Barry Mitchell, 'Minding the Gap in Unlawful and Dangerous Act Manslaughter: A Moral Defence of One-Punch Killers' (2008) 6(72) The Journal of Criminal Law 537

[446] Comodo (n 440); see also Microsoft Security Intelligence, 'Submit a file for malware analysis' (Microsoft Security Intelligence, 12th July 2017) <https://www.microsoft.com/en-us/wdsi/filesubmission> accessed 29 April 2019

It is common within the antivirus[447] and computer security industry[448] to keep registers of malicious code for the purpose of scanning client's computers and removing "malware"[449] and "nuisance-ware",[450] but this is predominantly a commercial industry in which the overall quality of each register will depend on the company that owns and maintains the register.[451] This would differ significantly from a government controlled and funded register,[452] which would have standards enforced by law. Another option could be to place the responsibility for this onto the companies that already produce these kinds of registers, by requiring them to update a central register.

In the instance of a national register for malicious code (NRMC) the government could keep an up to date register which programmers could submit their code to

---

[447] Melih Abdulhayoglu, 'The Need for a United Industry in Combating Malware' (2009) 9 Computer Fraud & Security 5

[448] Charles P Pfleeger and Shari Lawrence Pfleeger, *Analyzing Computer Security: A Threat/Vulnerability/Countermeasure Approach* (Prentice Hall Professional 2012) 8-16

[449] John Demme and others, 'On the Feasibility of Online Malware Detection with Performance Counters' (2013) 3(41) ACM SIGARCH Computer Architecture News 559

[450] Curtis E Karnow, 'Launch on Warning: Aggressive Defence of Computer Systems' (2005) 1(7) Yale Journal of Law & Technology 88

[451] Comodo (n 440); see also Microsoft (n 443)

[452] Multi-Agency Public Protection Arrangements, '8 ViSOR' (MAPPA Guidance, 5th September 2015) <https://mappa.justice.gov.uk/connect.ti/MAPPA/view?objectId=6854964> accessed 29 April 2019

prior to release[453] and that code could then be checked against code which had previously been identified as malicious or flawed.[454] Licencing requirements coupled with a NRMC could solve many future issues whilst also allowing the technology to be developed creatively and without unnecessary restraint. Requiring companies to be transparent with their own registers could create discontent within the private sector however, due to the profit that these industries generate from custom registers.[455]

The problems with a NRMC are that small variations in code could produce the same results and not be picked up by the register when a check was conducted, for this reason the register could offer a similarity grade to determine exactly how close of a match the submitted code was to previous malicious code, and a sandbox test where the code could be tested in a simulated environment similar to environments where code had been known to malfunction previously.[456] Ironically, machine learning could potentially be used to check code for issues[457] prior to deployment, potentially with much greater success.[458]

---

[453] cf Microsoft (n 443)

[454] *Clearswift Limited v Glasswall (IP) Limited* [2018] EWHC 2442

[455] Statista, 'Security software - Statistics & Facts' (Statista, 2nd April 2019) <https://www.statista.com/topics/2208/security-software/> accessed 29 April 2019

[456] Eike S Reetz and others, 'Test Driven Life Cycle Management for Internet of Things based Services: a Semantic Approach' (2012) The Fourth International Conference on Advances in System Testing and Validation Lifecycle 21

The combination of these tests would offer an early warning system for programmers but would also act as a form of foreseeability test[459] where a claim of GNM is made against a programmer. If another computer and multiple experts were unable to foresee any danger in the code then it would be much less likely for the foreseeability element of the *Adomako*[460] test to be satisfied. Foreseeability would undoubtedly be the most difficult element to satisfy due to the complexity of modern-day software,[461] OOP[462] allows programmers to work on small chunks of code at once, much like painting by number.

Moving onto a hardware-oriented perspective, there would be little point targeting legislation at programmers as they are usually responsible only for the programming.[463]

---

[457] Jesus Rodriguez, 'Machine Learning for Detecting Code Bugs' (Towards Data Science, 11 February 2019) <https://towardsdatascience.com/machine-learning-for-detecting-code-bugs-a79f37f144b7> accessed 27 April 2019

[458] Don Harris, *Engineering Psychology and Cognitive Ergonomics* (Springer 2015) 484

[459] Griffiths (n 314); see also Winterton (n 314); Mound (n 314); Matthew J Conigliaro, Andrew C Greenberg and Mark A Lemley, 'Foreseeability in Patent Law' (2001) 3(16) Berkeley Technology Law Journal 1045; Meikle (n 314)

[460] *Adomako* (n 6)

[461] Yutao Ma, Keqing He and Dehui Du, 'A qualitative method for measuring the structural complexity of software systems based on complex networks' (2005) APSEC'05 56

[462] Ole Lehrmann Madsen, Birger Møller-Pedersen and Kristen Nygaard, *Object-Oriented Programming in the Beta Programming Language* (Addison-Wesley 1993)

[463] Karen McCandless, 'What is Computer Programming?' (Code Academy, 13th June 2018) <https://news.codecademy.com/what-is-computer-

Instead the hardware architects[464] and the manufacturers[465] would be the logical choice, followed by the consumer. Where hardware is designed to maintain itself and produce copies of itself,[466] laws could be put into place requiring architects and manufacturers to be licenced and disclose certain information regarding the hardware that they are producing.[467] This solution could have a knock on effect with programmers as they would not be able to overcome hardware restrictions simply by programming a solution.

Punishing consumers for hardware misuse already appears to be a possibility, based on the wording of recent legislation. For example, the AEVA[468] discusses the liability of a person who should have installed "safety-critical" updates,[469] which overlaps with a software-oriented perspective. Essentially, software alterations cannot be made to an automated vehicle without approval by the manufacturer, and alterations that are safety critical must be installed.[470] This is primarily looked at from an

---

programming/> accessed 29 April 2019

[464] A Daneels and W Salter, 'What Is SCADA?' (1999) International Conference on Accelerator and Large Experimental Physics Control Systems 339

[465] Waymo (n 244)

[466] Gerard Briscoe and Paolo Dini, 'Towards Autopoietic Computing' [2010] London School of Economics and Political Science <https://arxiv.org/pdf/1009.0797.pdf> accessed 29 April 2019

[467] Gabriel Jacobs and Cliona O'Neill, 'On the reliability (or otherwise) of SIC codes' (2003) 3(15) European Business Review 164

[468] AEVA (n 72)

[469] ibid S4(6)(b)

insurance standpoint however,[471] not a criminality standpoint. The difference in perspective means that some situations are easily decided on, but others may still fall into a legal grey area.[472]

The second part of any criminal law solution is usually punishment.[473] In a situation where preventative measures have not worked and the law has been flaunted, it is necessary to consider the punishment. Sentences for GNM generally range from one to eighteen years in length[474] but may contain other stipulations such as a fine.[475] GNM is an indictable offence. In the case of GNM involving the use of AI, the punishment may need to be tailored more specifically to the particulars of the offence,[476] including who is being punished. Programmers would possibly need to be punished more severely than consumers.[477]

---

[470] ibid S4(4)(b)

[471] ibid S2

[472] Thomas F Gordon, 'An abductive theory of legal issues' 1 (1991) 35 International Journal of Man-Machine Studies 95

[473] Charles A Murray, *The Underclass Revisited* (American Enterprise Institute 1999)

[474] Sentencing Council, 'Sentencing guidelines for manslaughter introduced' (Sentencing Council, 31 July 2018) <https://www.sentencingcouncil.org.uk/news/item/sentencing-guidelines-for-manslaughter-introduced/> accessed 27 April 19

[475] Home Office, 'Reforming the Law on Involuntary Manslaughter: The Government's Proposals' (2000) Home Office Government Proposal Paper May 2000 <http://www.corporateaccountability.org.uk/dl/manslaughter/reform/archive/homeofficedraft2000.pdf> accessed 27 April 2019

[476] Orin S Kerr, *Computer Crime Law* (West 2009) 345-387

Consumers should be held to a basic standard, but generally a consumer would only have misused their own technology, meaning there is much less potential for widespread damage in cases of gross negligence. Depending on the subjective facts of the case,[477] consumers guilty of GNM in relation to AI should be handled under the standard sentencing guidelines for GNM.[479] It is unlikely that a consumer would be an expert in AI,[480] where that was not the case they should perhaps be handled as if they were a programmer or manufacturer. The status of 'consumer' could be considered a mitigating factor.[481]

Manufacturers are the halfway point between consumers and programmers, so whilst they are not usually experts in the finer details of the product that they are making and selling, they have more responsibility for their product than the consumer.[482] The responsibility of the manufacturer is also multiplied by the number of

---

[477] cf Sawicki (n 322)

[478] John Murungi, *An Introduction to African Legal Philosophy* (Lexington Books 2013) 147

[479] Steve Tombs, 'Still killing with impunity: corporate criminal law reform in the UK' (2013) 2(11) Policy and Practice in Health and Safety 63

[480] Leslie de Chernatony and Francesca Dall'Olmo Riley, 'The chasm between managers' and consumers' views of brands: the experts' perspectives' (1997) 2(5) Journal of Strategic Marketing 89

[481] Nick Barnard, 'Culpability and mitigation' (2016) 180(2) Criminal Law & Justice Weekly

[482] Gunkel (n 360) 36

consumers. They have an established duty[483] to each consumer to ensure that the product they are manufacturing, and selling, is safe.[484] For this reason, cases of GNM where the manufacturer is at fault should perhaps be handled slightly differently. The standard sentencing guidelines could be considered alongside other punishments.

Punishments which could be applied to the manufacturer could involve a ban on trading in AI enabled or related products,[485] a ban on developing or manufacturing those products or a ban on sitting as a director of any company that deals with those types of products.[486] These bans could be made permanent[487] or temporary.[488] The punishment should reflect the seriousness of the crime.[489] Manufacturers are also much more likely to be able to pay large fines, which consumers would in many cases struggle to afford.[490] This could be

[483] M Geistfeld 'Scientific Uncertainty and Causation in Tort Law.' (2001) 3(54) Vanderbilt Law Review 1011

[484] L Nancy Birnbaum, 'Strict Products Liability and Computer Software' (1988) 2(8) Computer Law Journal 135

[485] *McCluskey v North Lanarkshire Council* [2015] 11 WLUK 776

[486] Small Business, Enterprise and Employment Act 2015 S104-S116

[487] *Ineos Upstream Ltd v Lord Advocate* [2018] CSOH 66

[488] The Securitisation Regulations 2018 S21

[489] Deirdre Golash and James P Lynch, 'Public Opinion, Crime Seriousness, and Sentencing Policy' (1995) 3 (22) American Journal of Criminal Law 703

[490] Neil L Sobol, 'Fighting Fines & Fees: Borrowing from Consumer Law to Combat Criminal Justice Debt Abuses' (2017) 17-34 (88) University of Colorado Law Review 841

corporate manslaughter,[491] however, which is outside of the scope of this research.

Where a programmer if found guilty of GNM, they would more than likely be held to a much higher standard than consumers and manufacturers due to their expertise.[492] A programmer that has engaged in the creation of an AI should have been aware of the risks and methods of mitigating them,[493] otherwise it was a reckless engagement from the start.[494] Alongside the punishments that could be applied to consumers and manufacturers there are an array of punishments which could be specifically targeted at programmers. The purpose of these punishments would be to restrict a programmer's ability to reoffend in future.[495]

Programmers rely on access to certain programs and technology to create AI, as such programmers found guilty of GNM as a result of negligent coding could be banned from accessing a computer for a certain period.[496]

---

[491] Corporate Manslaughter and Corporate Homicide Act 2007

[492] Sawicki (n 322)

[493] Miles Brundage and others, 'The malicious use of artificial intelligence: Forecasting prevention and mitigation' (2018) University of Oxford <https://arxiv.org/ftp/arxiv/papers/1802/1802.07228.pdf> accessed 10 April 2019

[494] Alexander Sarch, 'Review of Findlay Stark, Culpable Carelessness: Recklessness and Negligence in the Criminal Law' (2017) 4(12) Criminal Law and Philosophy 725

[495] Richard S Frase, 'Punishment Purposes.' (2005) 1(58) Stanford Law Review 67

[496] Doug Hyne, 'Examining the Legal Challenges to the Restriction of Computer

They could also have their access to certain programs limited or be subject to observation or inspection.[497] These measures are already employed in certain cases involving serious sexual offences.[498] Registration as mentioned previously could be considered as a punishment in serious cases.[499] It would be important to set an example in each case to ensure due diligence from other programmers, otherwise history may repeat.

Punishment for the computer itself is the most difficult, in a hypothetical scenario where a computer could realise the consequences of its actions,[500] proving this would only be the first problem.[501] The more fundamental issue would arise when deciding how to punish the computer for its actions.[502] This is not something that could

Access as a Term of Probation or Supervised Release.' (2002) 2(28) New England Journal on Criminal and Civil Confinement 215

[497] Lars J Kangas and others, 'Computer-aided tracking and characterization of homicides and sexual assaults (CATCH)' (1999) Proc SPIE 3722, Applications and Science of Computational Intelligence II

[498] Ian A Elliot, Donald Findlater and Teresa Hughes, 'Practice report: A review of e-Safety remote' (2010) 16(2) Journal of Sexual Aggression 237

[499] Velmer S Burton and others, 'The Collateral Consequences of a Felony Conviction: A National Study of State Statutes' (1987) 51(3) Federal probation 52

[500] Burton Voorhees, 'Gödel's theorem and the possibility of thinking machines: Do androids dream of electric sheep?' (1995) 1(3) Complexity 30

[501] Stuart Russell, Daniel Dewey and Max Tegmark, 'Research Priorities for Robust and Beneficial Artificial Intelligence' (2015) 4(36) AI Magazine 105

[502] Ann W Branscomb, 'Rogue Computer Programs and Computer Rogues: Tailoring the Punishment to Fit the Crime' (1990) 16(1) Rutgers Computer & Tech Law Journal 1

be decided definitively at this point in history, although it may become necessary in coming years to look more closely at the relationship between computers, human understanding of consciousness and their relationship with the law.[503] Computers that could understand their actions would need to be punishable, however.[504]

Where computers are found to understand their actions, and where they satisfy the requirements of *Adomako*[505] to the point where they can be found guilty of GNM as a separate individual, there are several punishments that Parliament could consider imposing. The standard punishment initially would more than likely be digital-capital-punishment, deleting the offending mind,[506] as controversial as it would likely be.[507] Other options that could be considered do include retraining[508] and

---

[503] Steven Goldberg, 'The Changing Face of Death: Computers, Consciousness, and Nancy Cruzan' (1991) 43(3) Stanford Law Review 659

[504] Richard Sparks, *The SAGE Handbook of Punishment and Society* (SAGE 2012) 23-24

[505] *Adomako* (n 6)

[506] Henry T Greely, 'Neuroscience and Criminal Justice: Not Responsibility but Treatment' (2008) 56(5) Kansas Law Review 1103

[507] William O Hochkammer, 'Capital Punishment Controversy' (1970) 60(3) Journal of Criminal Law and Criminology 360

[508] Judith M Collins and Murray R Clark, 'An Application of the Theory of Neural Computation to the Prediction of Workplace Behavior: An Illustration and Assessment of Network Analysis' (1993) 3(46) Personnel Psychology 503; see also Clyde B Vedder, 'Florida Prison Pioneers Academic In-Service Training,' (1954) 1954 Proceedings of the Annual Congress of Correction of the American Prison Association 60

rehabilitation[509] or rewriting,[510] however. The latter of which offers an interesting perspective on the reform of offenders,[511] especially in contrast to human offenders, due to the more precise science.[512]

For example, if a computer was undertaking a particularly harmful action due to a specific memory,[513] that memory could be digitally removed,[514] and new memories could be created which could have the effect of altering specific aspects of the computer's behaviour. Computers that place too much emphasis on a goal,[515] could be manually modified programmatically to ensure that they placed more emphasis on other goals and more desirable traits.[516] In any case however, the pessimistic belief that AI

---

[509] R Blackburn, *The psychology of criminal conduct: Theory, research and practice* (John Wiley & Sons 1993)

[510] Ejike Ofuonye and James Miller, 'Securing web-clients with instrumented code and dynamic runtime monitoring' (2013) 6(86) The Journal of Systems and Software 1689

[511] Steven Hutchinson, 'Countering catastrophic criminology: Reform, punishment and the modern liberal compromise' (2006) 4(8) Punishment & Society 443

[512] Andrew Hugill, 'Introduction: transdisciplinary learning for digital creative practice' (2013) 3(24) Digital Creativity 165

[513] Gunnar Schulze, 'Neural Networks, Brain Bugs and Deep Learning' (Norbis, 20th June 2016) <https://norbis.w.uib.no/blog/neural-networks-brain-bugs-and-deep-learning/> accessed 29 April 2019

[514] MY Rafiq, G Bugmann and DJ Easterbrook, 'Neural network design for engineering applications' (2001) 17(79) Computers and Structures 1541

[515] Schulze (n 510)

[516] Yves Chauvin and David E Rumelhart, *Backpropagation: Theory, Architectures and Applications* (Psychology Press 2013)

will one day result in the end of humanity has already been expressed by several scientists,[517] including the late Professor Stephen Hawking.[518]

---

[517] Benjamin Bathke, 'Artificial intelligence, or the end of the world as we know it' (Deutsche Welle, 26th October 2018) <https://www.dw.com/cda/en/artificial-intelligence-ai-automation-technology-harari-machine-learning-ethics-obama-future-oslo/a-45932260> accessed 14 April 2019

[518] Stephen Hawking and others, 'Stephen Hawking: 'Transcendence looks at the implications of artificial intelligence - but are we taking AI seriously enough?'' (Independent, 1st May 2014) <https://www.independent.co.uk/news/science/stephen-hawking-transcendence-looks-at-the-implications-of-artificial-intelligence-but-are-we-taking-9313474.html> accessed 14 April 2019

## 4. Conclusion

In conclusion, AI is a vast and expanding industry,[519] which encroaches more on society with every passing day. Banning AI would likely have little effect on its development due to the scale of the current industry[520] and the availability of compatible technology,[521] as such statutory regulation is the most viable way forward. Regulation of the industry should be a key goal for Parliament in coming years, specifically with a focus on intentional[522] and unintentional[523] criminal misuse, followed by a focus on other areas.[524] Parliament will need to consider the broader impact of any restrictions placed on both hardware and software.

Software restrictions should be considered in the form of licencing for manufacturers[525] and there should be

---

[519] Charlotte A Tschider 'Deus Ex Machina: Regulating Cybersecurity and Intelligence for Patients of the Future' [2018] 5(1) Savannah Law Review 177

[520] Nathan Collins, 'How artificial intelligence is changing science' (Stanford News, 15th May 2018) <https://news.stanford.edu/2018/05/15/how-ai-is-changing-science/> accessed 19 April 2019

[521] Thomas H Spotts, 'Discriminating Factors in Faculty Use of Instructional Technology on Higher Education' (1999) 2(4) Educational Technology & Society 92

[522] Gabriel Hallevy, *When Robots Kill: Artificial Intelligence Under Criminal Law* (Northeastern University Press 2013) 80

[523] SM Solaiman, 'Liability for industrial manslaughter caused by robots under statutory laws in Australia' [2017] 38(7) Company Law 226

[524] Andrew J Wu, 'From Video Games to Artificial Intelligence: Assigning Copyright Ownership to Works Generated by Increasingly Sophisticated Computer Programs' (1997) 25(1) AIPLA Quarterly Journal 131

[525] Misuse of Drugs Act 1971 S7(3)(a); see also Alcoholic Liquor Duties Act

more support for programmers that wish to ensure that they will not be prosecuted for unintentional code faults.[526] This can be done in a variety of ways, but a government database[527] or testing agency[528] which checks programs for a fee would potentially be the best option. Registration for offenders should be handled delicately, if at all, and only as a final resort to not discourage development and scientific advancement.[529] Expert advice should be considered before any action is taken due to the industries' complexity.[530]

Hardware related legislation should be considered in conjunction with software related legislation for a more complete response to the issues.[531] Legislation may be targeted more at manufacturers;[532] this could be done by requiring redundancies to be built into machines so that in

1979 S12

[526] Richard T De George, *The Ethics of Information Technology and Business* (2nd edn, John Wiley & Sons 2008) 10

[527] Tara Lamont and Others, 'Reducing risks of tourniquets left on after finger and toe surgery: summary of a safety report from the National Patient Safety Agency' [2010] c1981 340 BMJ 973

[528] James A Jones, Mark Grechanik and Andre van der Hoek, 'Enabling and Enhancing Collaborations between Software Development Organizations and Independent Test Agencies' (2009) ICSE Workshop on Cooperative and Human Aspects on Software Engineering 56

[529] JW Dornseiffen, 'Residue aspects of disinfectants used in the food industry' (1998) 41(3-4) International Biodeterioration & Biodegradation 309

[530] Kenneth Flamm, *Creating the Computer: Government, Industry, and High Technology* (Brookings Institution Press 1988) 1-7

[531] Police and Justice Act 2006 S37

[532] ALDA (n 522) S12

case of systems failure they default to a safe state. Asimov's consideration of this in science fiction,[533] through his three laws of robotics,[534] is an interesting perspective which could be modified more realistically for use in areas such as the AV industry. For example, the AV may have a secondary controller which prioritises the protection of human life.

Preventing a scenario where an autopoietic or intelligent machine[535] makes a poor decision resulting in the death of a person[536] is going to be difficult due to the rapid expansion of the industry and its uses. Ultimately it will be the legislatures responsibility to avoid placing the courts in a position where they must decide on a case like this without the guidance of clear legislation, Parliament should target possible scenarios with appropriate legislation. The AEVA[537] was an important step towards preventing issues arising civilly but more must be done in future to avoid the issues which may arise criminally.

Lastly, due consideration must be given to whom, and how, a punishment could apply.[538] For this to be done

---

[533] Isaac Asimov, *I, Robot* (Bantam Books 2004)

[534] Jacob Turner, *Robot Rules: Regulating Artificial Intelligence* (Springer 2018) 1-2

[535] Kaplan (n 2); see also Flett (n 2)

[536] Levin (n 248)

[537] AEVA (n 72)

[538] Technology (n 269)

correctly it would be necessary to first assess causation;[539] if the consumer was at fault then the case could proceed as a standard case of GNM,[540] where the programmer was responsible then this would likely add weight to an argument of professional GNM,[541] where the manufacturer was responsible the case could fall into the scope of corporate manslaughter[542] and in the unfortunate event that the software was found to be at fault, this may eventually develop into a new offence entirely.

Ultimately the law must adapt and grow alongside technology, because both have become integral elements of modern society, and while technology may be the younger of the two, both are equal in permanence. It will be interesting to see how this relationship develops over the coming years, but certainly there will need to be much more work done before the relationship can achieve symbiosis. This research is in no way intended to be a complete summary of the contemporary issues, but hopefully it has been thought provoking. Perhaps eventually, a machine will be capable of analysing these issues for itself.

---

539 *Zaman* (n 315) 38
540 *Adomako* (n 6)
541 *Bawa-Garba* (n 321)
542 CMCHA (n 488)

# Appendices

## Appendix A – Central Processing Unit (CPU) Speed

This table compares a range of CPU's from 1971 to 2017, with the human brain.

| Name | Max Speed (Hz) | Cores | Bits | Release Date | Link |
|------|------|------|------|------|------|
| Intel 4004 | 740,000 | 1 | 4 | 15/11/1971 | 543 |
| Intel 80386 SX | 16,000,000 | 1 | 16 | 06/1988 | 544 |
| AMD AM386 * | 40,000,000 | 1 | 32 | 03/1991 | 545 |
| Intel Pentiu | 150,000,00 0 | 1 | 32 | 11/1995 | 546 |

543 Intel, 'The Story of the Intel® 4004: Intel's First Microprocessor' (Intel, Unknown Date) <https://www.intel.co.uk/content/www/uk/en/history/museum-story-of-intel-4004.html> accessed 03 November 2018

544 University of British Columbia, 'The 80386SX Processor Bus and Real-Mode Instruction Set' (EECE 379: design of digital and microcomputer systems, 2000) <http://www.ece.ubc.ca/~edc/379/lectures/lec2.pdf> accessed 04 November 2018

545 Hardware Museum, 'AMD AM386 DXL-40' (Hardware Museum, 28th November 2018) <http://hw-museum.cz/cpu/130/amd-am386-dxl-40> accessed 02 December 2018

546 Intel, 'Intel® Pentium® Processor 150 MHz, 60 MHz FSB' (Intel Support, November 1995) <https://ark.intel.com/products/49958/Intel-Pentium-Processor-150-MHz-60-MHz-FSB> accessed 01 December 2018

| | | | | | |
|---|---|---|---|---|---|
| m | | | | | |
| Intel Celeron | 800,000,000 | 1 | 32 | 03/01/2001 | [547] |
| Intel i5-750 | 3,200,000,000 | 4 | 64 | 08/09/2009 | [548] |
| AMD A10-5800K | 4,200,000,000 | 4 | 64 | 01/10/2012 | [549] |
| AMD FX-8350 | 4,200,000,000 | 8 | 64 | 23/10/2012 | [550] |
| Intel Core i7- | 4,200,000,000 | 4 | 64 | 22/04/2014 | [551] |

---

[547] Intel, 'Intel® Celeron® Processor 800 MHz, 128K Cache, 100 MHz FSB' (Intel Support, January 2001) <https://ark.intel.com/products/27197/Intel-Celeron-Processor-800-MHz-128K-Cache-100-MHz-FSB> accessed 01 December 2018

[548] Intel, 'Intel® Core™ i5-750 Processor' (Intel Support, September 2009) <https://ark.intel.com/products/42915/Intel-Core-i5-750-Processor-8M-Cache-2-66-GHz-> accessed 01 December 2018

[549] PassMark Software, 'CPU Benchmarks: AMD A10-5800K APU' (PassMark Software, October 2012) <https://www.cpubenchmark.net/cpu.php?cpu=AMD+A10-5800K+APU&id=1446> accessed 02 December 2018

[550] Amazon, 'AMD FX 8350 Black Edition "Vishera" CPU (8 Core, AM3+, Clock 4.0 GHz, Turbo 4.2 GHz, 8 MB L3 Cache, 125 W)' (Amazon.co.uk, 22nd April 2014) <http://amzn.eu/d/hanfQom> accessed 12 October 2018

[551] Amazon, 'Intel i7-7700K Quad Core 4.2GHz LGA1151 HD 630 8MB Intel HD Graphics Cache 91W TDP CPU Processor' (Amazon.co.uk, 23rd October 2012) <https://www.amazon.co.uk/Intel-i7-7700K-LGA1151-Graphics-Processor/dp/B01LTI1JEM/> accessed 13 October 2018

| 7700K | | | | | |
|---|---|---|---|---|---|
| Intel Core i9 7980X E | 4,400,000, 000 | 18 | 64 | 18/08/2017 | [552] |
| The Huma n Brain | 5 to 1000 (10avg)[553] | 86,000, 000,000[55] | N/A | N/A | [**] |

*The AMD AM386 was released a few months after the Computer Misuse Act 1990.

**The human brain is largely incomparable with a computer processing unit (CPU), but neurons could be viewed as individual cores operating in parallel and the speed of each neuron in hertz could then be compared to the speed of a CPU core.

[552] Intel, 'Intel® Core™ I9-7980XE Extreme Edition Processor' (Intel, August 2017) <https://www.intel.co.uk/content/www/uk/en/products/processors/core/x-series/i9-7980xe.html> accessed 02 December 2018

[553] Bernard J Baars and Nicole M Gage, Cognition, Brain, And Consciousness: Introduction to Cognitive Neuroscience (2nd edn, Academic Press 2010) 7

[554] Suzana Herculano-Houzel, 'The Human Brain in Numbers: A Linearly Scaled-up Primate Brain' [2009] 31(3) Frontiers in Human Neuroscience 7

## Appendix B – Legislation Release Dates

This table compares the release dates of relevant legislation.

| Title | Years and Numbers | Citation |
|---|---|---|
| **Computer Misuse Act 1990** | 1990 c.18 | [555] |
| **Automated and Electric Vehicles Act 2018** | 2018 c.18 | [556] |

---

[555] Computer Misuse Act 1990
[556] Automated and Electric Vehicles Act 2018

Appendix C – German Law

This table displays German legislation with translations which may be difficult for the reader to find independently.

| Section | German | English |
|---|---|---|
| **§ 7 UrhG (Urheberrechtsgesetz) (Copyright Act)** | Urheber - Urheber ist der Schöpfer des Werkes.[557] | Author - Author is the creator of the work. |

---

[557] Dejure, 'Urheberrechtsgesetz' (Dejure, 19th March 2019) <https://dejure.org/gesetze/UrhG/7.html> accessed 19 March 2019

Bibliography

Legislation

Alcoholic Liquor Duties Act 1979

Automated and Electric Vehicles Act 2018

Children Act 1989

Children and Young Persons Act 1933

Companies Act 2006

Computer Misuse Act 1990

Copyright, Designs and Patents Act 1988

Corporate Manslaughter and Corporate Homicide Act 2007

Corporation Tax Act 2010

Criminal Justice Act 1982

Criminal Justice Act 2003

Diplomatic Privileges Act 1964

Equality Act 2010

Forfeiture Act 1982

Government of Wales Act 2006

Human Rights Act 1998

International Criminal Court Act 2001

Licensing Act 2003

Mental Health Act 1983

Misuse of Drugs Act 1971

Pensions Act 2004

Private Hire Vehicles (London) Act 1998

Private Security Industry Act 2001

Road Traffic Act 1988

Police and Justice Act 2006

Sexual Offences Act 2003

Small Business, Enterprise and Employment Act 2015

The Export of Goods (Control) Order 1989

The Motor Vehicles (Driving Licences) Regulations 1999

The Securitisation Regulations 2018

Union with England Act 1707


Legislation (European Union)

Convention for the Protection of Human Rights and Fundamental Freedoms (European Convention on Human Rights, as amended) (ECHR)

Legislation (United States of America)

17 U.S.C §□101-1401 (1976)

5 U.S.C §□3110 (2006)

Cases

*Alcock and Others v Chief Constable of South Yorkshire Police* [1991] 3 W.L.R. 1057

*Amir Khan v Muhammad Zubair Hussain* [2019] CSOH 11

*Andrew Winterton v Regina* [2018] EWCA Crim 2435

*Anns and Others v Merton London Borough Council* [1977] 2 W.L.R. 1024, 734

*Attorney General's Reference (No.2 of 1999)* [2000] Q.B. 796

*Bourhill v Young* [1943] A.C. 92

*Brown v Paterson* [2010] EWCA Civ 184, 3

*BSkyB Limited, Sky Subscribers Services Limited v HP Enterprise Services UK Limited (formerly Electronic Data Systems Limited), Electronic Data systems LLC (Formerly Electronic Data Systems Corporation)* [2010] EWHC 86 (TCC)

*Cantor Fitzgerald International v Tradition (UK) Ltd. & Ors* [1999] WL 1048259

*Caparo Industries Plc. v Dickman and Others* [1990] 2 W.L.R. 358

*Christian Connor v Regina* [2019] EWCA Crim 234

*Clark v Farley* [2018] EWHC 1007 (QB)

*Clearswift Limited v Glasswall (IP) Limited* [2018] EWHC 2442

*Cummins v Bond* [1927] 1 Ch. 167

*Director of Public Prosecutions v Heywood* [1998] R.T.R. 1

*Donoghue v Stevenson* [1932] AC 562

*Gillick v West Norfolk and Wisbech Area Health Authority and Department of Health and Social Security* [1985] 3 W.L.R. 830

*Gooda Walker Ltd. (In Liquidation) and Others v Deeny and Others* [1994] 3 W.L.R. 761, 150-151

*Gujra v Roath and another* [2018] 1 W.L.R. 3208

*Hadiza Bawa-Garba v The General Medical Council v The British Medical Association, The Professional Standards Authority for Health and Social Care, The British Association of Physicians of Indian Origin* [2018] EWCA Civ 1879

*Hill v Chief Constable of West Yorkshire* [1989] A.C. 53

*Home Office v Dorset Yacht Co. Ltd.* [1970] 2 W.L.R. 1140

*In the Matter of Kent County Council v [Adult A], [Adult B], [Adult C], [Adult D]* [2017] WL 06806128, 95

*Ineos Upstream Ltd v Lord Advocate* [2018] CSOH 66

*James Douglas Ferguson v Her Majesty's Advocate* [2014] HCJAC 19

*Jessica Griffiths, Hannah Griffiths, Sophie Griffiths, (A minor by her father and Litigation Friend Jeremy Griffiths) v The Chief*

*Constable of the Suffolk Police, Norfolk and Suffolk NHS Foundation Trust* [2018] EWHC 2538 (QB)

*L (A Child)* [2019] WL 00937194

*Lauri Love v The National Crime Agency* [2019] 2 WLUK 464

*Love v Government of the United States of America (Liberty intervening)* [2018] 1 W.L.R. 2889

*McCluskey v North Lanarkshire Council* [2015] 11 WLUK 776

*McKinnon v Government of the United States of America* [2008] 1 W.L.R. 1739

*McLaughlin v Morrison* [2014] S.L.T. 111

*McQuire v Western Morning News Company, Limited* [1903] 2 K.B. 100, 109

*NCC v PB (By her litigation friend the Official Solicitor), TB (By his litigation friend the Official Solicitor)* [2014] EWCOP 14

*North West Anglia NHS Foundation Trust v Dr Andrew Gregg* [2019] EWCA Civ 387

*Overseas Tankship (U.K.) Ltd v Morts Dock & Engineering Co Ltd (the Wagon Mound)* [1961] A.C. 388

*Polemis v Furness Withy & Co* [1921] 3 K.B. 560

*Pook v Rossall School* [2018] EWHC 522 (QB)

*Privacy International v Secretary of State for Foreign and Commonwealth Affairs, Secretary of State for the Home Department, Government Communications Headquarters,*

Security Service, Secret Intelligence Service [2018] 4 All E.R. 275

Privacy International v Secretary of State for Foreign and Commonwealth Affairs [2016] H.R.L.R. 21

R (on the application of Salman Butt) v The Secretary of State for the Home Department [2019] EWCA Civ 256

R v Gurphal Singh [1999] Crim LR 582

R v Mohammed Khalique Zaman [2017] EWCA Crim 1783

R. (on the application of Rowley) v DPP [2003] EWHC 693

R. v Adomako [1994] 3 WLR 288

R. v Connolly (Mark Anthony) [2007] EWCA Crim 790

R. v Connor Douglas Allsopp [2019] EWCA Crim 95

R. v DPP Ex p. Jones (Timothy) [2000] I.R.L.R. 373

R. v Evans [2009] 1 W.L.R. 1999

R. v Johnson (Wayne) [2018] 1 W.L.R. 19

R. v Lane and another [2018] 1 W.L.R. 3647

R. v M (D) and another [2011] 1 W.L.R. 822

R. v Misra and Srivastava [2005] 1 Cr. App. R. 21

R. v Mudd [2017] EWCA Crim 1395

R. v Paul Anthony Finlay [2003] EWCA Crim 3868

R. v Wacker [2002] EWCA Crim 1944

*Regina (Birks) v Commissioner of Police of the Metropolis and another (No 2)* [2018] I.C.R. 1400

*Regina (Medical Justice and others) v Secretary of State for the Home Department (Equality and Human Rights Commission intervening)* [2017] 4 W.L.R. 198

*Regina v Imtiaz Hussain* [2006] EWCA Crim 1372

*Regina v Liam Holgate* [2019] EWCA Crim 338

*Rory Davis v George Fessey, Leisure Ninety Nine Limited, West Yorkshire Security UK Limited, Ian Cox (Trading as Cox Security Services)* [2018] 4 WLUK 29

*Various Claimants v Wm Morrison Supermarkets plc* [2019] 2 W.L.R. 99

*Wang Laboratories Inc.'s Application* [1991] R.P.C. 463

*Wembridge v Winter* [2013] EWHC 2331 (QB)

*X v Bedfordshire* [1995] 2 A.C. 633


Cases (United States of America)

*Garnett v State* 332 Md. 571 (Md. 1993)

*Naruto v Slater*, No. 16-15469 (9th Cir. 2018)

Books

Abbot C, *Enforcing Pollution Control Regulation: Strengthening Sanctions and Improving Deterrence* (Bloomsbury Publishing 2009)

Agah A, *Medical Applications of Artificial Intelligence* (1st edn, CRC Press 6th November 2013)

Ahmed H and Spreadbury PJ, *Analogue and digital electronics for engineers: An Introduction* (Cambridge University Press 1984)

Alpaydin E, *Introduction to Machine Learning* (3rd edn, MIT Press 2014)

Alpaydin E, *Machine Learning: The New AI* (1st edn, MIT Press 2016)

Ashworth A, Zedner L and Tomlin P, *Prevention and the Limits of the Criminal Law* (Oxford University Press 2013)

Asimov I, *I, Robot* (Bantam Books 2004)

Baars BJ and Gage NM, *Cognition, Brain, And Consciousness: Introduction to Cognitive Neuroscience* (2nd edn, Academic Press 2010)

Babbage C, *Passages from The life of a Philosopher* (Longman, Green, Longman, Roberts & Green 1864)

Baldauf S, *Instructor Edition: Succeeding with Technology 2005 Update* (Course Technology 2005)

Ball H, *The Right to Die: A Reference Handbook* (ABC-CLIO 2017)

Ballard DH, *Brain Computation as Hierarchical Abstraction* (MIT Press 2015)

Basak A, *Analogue electronic circuits and systems* (Cambridge University Press 1991)

Blackburn R, *The psychology of criminal conduct: Theory, research and practice* (John Wiley & Sons 1993)

Bradley R, *Understanding Computing AS Level for AQA* (Nelson Thornes 2004)

Buchanan AE, *The Evolution of Moral Progress: A Biocultural Theory* (Oxford University Press 2018)

Carcieri MD, *Applying Rawls in the Twenty-First Century: Race, Gender, The Drug War and the Right to Die* (Palgrave Macmillan 2015)

Carvalho H, *The Preventive Turn in Criminal Law* (Oxford University Press 2017)

Chalmers DJ, *The Conscious Mind: In Search of a Fundamental Theory* (Oxford University Press USA 1997)

Chauvin Y and Rumelhart DE, *Backpropagation: Theory, Architectures and Applications* (Psychology Press 2013)

Chen Q, *Cellular Automata and Artificial Intelligence in Ecohydraulics Modelling* (1st edn, CRC Press 2004)

Chen Q, *Governance, Social Control and Legal Reform in China: Community Sanctions and Measures* (Springer 2018)

Collier B and MacLachlan J, *Charles Babbage and the Engines of Perfection* (Oxford University Press 1998)

Copeland BJ, *Alan Turing's Automatic Computing Engine: The Master Codebreaker's Struggle to Build the Modern Computer* (Oxford University Press 2005)

Craig WL and Moreland JP, *The Blackwell Companion to Natural Theology* (Wiley-Blackwell 2009)

Crane T and Patterson S, *History of the Mind-Body Problem* (Routledge 2000)

Crockett LJ, *The Turing Test and the Frame Problem: AI's Mistaken Understanding of Intelligence* (Ablex Publishing Corporation 1994)

Damer TE, *Attacking Faulty Reasoning: A Practical Guide to Fallacy-Free Arguments* (6th edn, Wadsworth Cengage Learning 2009)

Davis SR and Sphar C, *C# 2005 for Dummies* (Wiley Publishing 2006)

De George RT, *The Ethics of Information Technology and Business* (2nd edn, John Wiley & Sons 2008)

DeCasare M, *Death on Demand: Jack Kevorkian and the Right to Die Movement* (Rowman and Littlefield 2015)

Dershowitz AM, *Preemption: A Knife That Cuts Both Ways* (WW Norton & Company 2006)

Descartes R, *Discourse on Method of Rightly Conducting One's Reason and of Seeking Truth in the Sciences* (CreateSpace Independent Publishing Platform, 14th July 2017)

Dimitrakos T and others, *Formal Aspects in Security and Trust: Third International Workshop, FAST 2005, Newcastle upon Tyne, UK, July 18-19, 2005, Revised Selected Papers* (Springer 2006)

Domeika M, *Software Development for Embedded Multi-core Systems: A Practical Guide Using Embedded Intel ® Architecture* (Elsevier 2008)

Donkin S, *Preventing Terrorism and Controlling Risk: A Comparative Analysis of Control Orders in the UK and Australia* (Springer Science & Business Media 2013)

Earman J, *A primer on Determinism* (D Reidel 1986)

Eisner C and Vicinus M, *Originality, Imitation, and Plagiarism: Teaching Writing in the Digital Age* (The University of Michigan 2008)

Eliasmith C and Anderson CH, *Computational Neuroscience: Computation, Representation and Dynamics in Neurobiological Systems* (The MIT Press 2003)

Ellacott SW, Mason JC and Anderson IJ, *Mathematics of Neural Networks: Models, Algorithms and Applications* (Springer Science & Business Media 1997)

Epstein R, *Parsing the Turing Test: Philosophical and Methodological Issues in the Quest for the Thinking Computer* (Springer 2008)

Essinger J, *Ada's Algorithm: How lord Byron's Daughter Launched the Digital Age* (Gibson Square 2013)

Evans CL, *Broad Band: The Untold Story of the Women Who Made the Internet* (Penguin 2018)

Farthing GW, *The Psychology of Consciousness* (Prentice Hall 1992)

Feintuck M and Whitehouse M, *'The Public Interest' in Regulation* (Oxford University Press 2004)

Ferri F, *Visual Languages for Interactive Computing: Definitions and Formalizations* (Idea Group Inc (IGI) 2008)

Flamm K, *Creating the Computer: Government, Industry, and High Technology* (Brookings Institution Press 1988)

Fletcher GP, *Rethinking Criminal Law* (Oxford University Press 2000)

Freitas RA and Merkle RC, *Kinematic Self-Replicating Machines* (Landes Bioscience 2004)

Gardner H, *Frames of Mind: The theory of multiple intelligences* (2nd edn, Basic Books 1993)

Gay DM, *Correctly Rounded Binary-Decimal and Decimal-Binary Conversions* (AT&T Bell Laboratories 1990)

Gluck MA and Myers CE, *Gateway to Memory: An Introduction to Neural Network Modeling of the Hippocampus and Learning* (A Bradford Book 2001)

Greenawalt K, *Statutory and Common Law Interpretation* (Oxford University Press 2013)

Gruner RS, *Corporate Criminal Liability and Prevention* (Law Journal Press 2004)

Gulli A and Pal S, *Deep Learning with Keras* (Packt Publishing Ltd 2017)

Gunkel DJ, *The Machine Question: Critical Perspectives on AI, Robots, and Ethics* (MIT Press 2012)

Guttenplan S, *A Companion to the Philosophy of Mind* (Blackwell Publishers 1994)

Haikonen PO, *Consciousness and Robot Sentience* (World Scientific Publishing Co 2012)

Hallevy G, *When Robots Kill: Artificial Intelligence Under Criminal Law* (Northeastern University Press 2013)

Hammerstein P, *Genetic and Cultural Evolution of Cooperation* (MIT Press 2003)

Harel A and Hylton KN, *Research Handbook on the Economics of Criminal Law* (Edward Elgar Publishing 2012)

Harris D, *Engineering Psychology and Cognitive Ergonomics* (Springer 2015)

Hayder H, *Object-Oriented Programming with PHP5* (Packt Publishing 2007)

Hergenhahn B, *An Introduction to the History of Psychology* (Cengage Learning 2004)

Hogan GW and Walker C, *Political Violence and the Law in Ireland* (Manchester University Press 1989)

Holland O, *Machine Consciousness* (Imprint Academic 2003)

Huxley-Binns R, *Criminal Law Concentrate* (Oxford University Press 2014)

Jamil T, *Complex Binary Number System: Algorithms and Circuits* (Springer 2013)

Kendal S, *Object Oriented Programming using Java* (Ventus Publishing 2009)

Kerr OS, *Computer Crime Law* (West 2009)

Konar A, *Artificial Intelligence and Soft Computing: Behavioural and Cognitive Modelling of the Human Brain* (1st edn, CRC Press 8th December 1999)

Kuiken TA, Feuser AES and Barlow AK, *Targeted Muscle Reinnervation: A Neural Interface for Artificial Limbs* (1st edn, CRC Press 23rd July 2013).

Kwok J, Zhang L and Lu B, *Advances in Neural Networks -- ISNN 2010: 7th International Symposium on Neural Networks, ISNN 2010, Shanghai, China, June 6-9, 2010, Proceedings* (Springer Science & Business Media, 20 May 2010)

Lafore R, *Object-Oriented Programming in C++* (4th edn, Sams Publishing 2002)

Leavitt D, *The Man Who Knew Too Much: Alan Turing and the invention of computers* (1st edn, Weidenfeld & Nicolson 22nd January 2015)

Leondes CT, *Neural Network Systems Techniques and Applications: Control and Dynamic Systems* (Academic Press 1998)

Lipson H and Kurman M, *Driverless: Intelligent Cars and the Road Ahead* (1st edn, MIT Press 4th October 2016)

Livingstone EA, *The Oxford Dictionary of the Christian Church* (3rd edn, Oxford University Press 1997)

Lloyd I, *Information Technology Law* (Oxford University Press 2017)

Luria AR, *Cortical Functions in Man* (Basic Books 1966)

Madsen OL, Møller-Pedersen B and Nygaard K, *Object-Oriented Programming in the Beta Programming Language* (Addison-Wesley 1993)

Marshak DR, Gottlieb D and Gardner RL, *Stem Cell Biology* (Cold Spring Harbour Laboratory Press 2000)

Martone LI, *Giamblico De Anima I frammenti la dottrina* (Pisa University Press 2014)

Masters T, *Practical Neural Network Recipes in C++* (Academic Press 1993)

Maturana HR and Varela FJ, *Autopoiesis and Cognition: The Realization of the Living* (1st edn, D. Reidel Publishing Company 1980)

Millington I, *Artificial Intelligence for Games* (1st edn, CRC Press 28th July 2006)

Müller VC, *Risks of Artificial Intelligence* (1st edn, Chapman and Hall/CRC 10th December 2015)

Murch R, *The Software Development Lifecycle - A Complete Guide* (Amazon.co.uk 2012)

Murray CA, *The Underclass Revisited* (American Enterprise Institute 1999)

Murungi J, *An Introduction to African Legal Philosophy* (Lexington Books 2013)

Nagel T, *Mortal Questions* (Cambridge University Press 1979)

Naguib RNG and Sherbet GV, *Artificial Neural Networks in Cancer Diagnosis, Prognosis, and Patient Management* (1st edn, CRC Press 2001)

Neapolitan RE and Jiang X, *Artificial Intelligence: With an introduction to Machine Learning* (2nd edn, CRC Press 2018)

Neuwirth S, *Learning Disabilities* (Diane Publishing 1993)

Norris DJ, *Beginning Artificial Intelligence with the Raspberry Pi* (Apress 2017)

Organisation for Economic Coordination and Development, *Understanding the Brain: The Birth of a Learning Science* (OECD 2007)

Oxford University Press, *Oxford Advanced Learner's Dictionary* (8th edn, Oxford University Press 21st August 2012)

Parsons JJ, *New Perspectives Computer Concepts 2016 Enhanced, Comprehensive* (Cengage Learning 2016)

Pascual DG, *Artificial Intelligence Tools: Decision Support Systems in Condition Monitoring and Diagnosis* (1st edn, CRC Press 22nd April 2015)

Patterson DA and Hennessy JL, *Computer Organization and Design: The Hardware/Software Interface* (Morgan Kaufmann 2008)

Peter Dayan and L.F. Abbott, *Theoretical Neuroscience* (The MIT Press 2001)

Peter S Eardley and Carl N Still, *Aquinas: A Guide for the Perplexed* (Bloomsbury 2010)

Pfleeger CP and Pfleeger SL, *Analyzing Computer Security: A Threat/Vulnerability/Countermeasure Approach* (Prentice Hall Professional 2012)

Piaget J, *The Psychology of Intelligence* (Armand Colin 1947)

Polansky R, *Aristotle's De Anima* (Cambridge University Press 2007)

Poo D, Kiong D and Ashok S, *Object-Oriented Programming and Java* (2nd edn, Springer 2008)

R S Soin, F Maloberti and J Franca, *Analogue to Digital ASICs: circuit techniques, design tools and applications* (Peter Peregrinus 1991)

Reed WE, *The Politics of Community Policing: The Case of Seattle* (Routledge 2013)

Reinders J, *Intel Threading Building Blocks Outfitting C++ for Multi-Core Processor Parallelism* (O'Reilly Media 2007)

Robinson G and McNeill F, *Community Punishment: European perspectives* (Routledge 2015)

Rosenfield B, *Assisted Suicide and The Right To Die: The Interface of Social Science, Public Policy, and Medical Ethics* (American Psychology Association 2004)

Rudomin P and others, *Neuroscience: From Neural Networks to Artificial Intelligence: Proceedings of a U.S.-Mexico Seminar held in the city of Xalapa in the state of Veracruz on December 9–11, 1991* (Springer Science & Business Media 2012)

Russell SJ and others, Artificial Intelligence: A Modern Approach (3rd edn, Harlow Pearson Education cop. 2016) pp1024-1026

Salomon D, *Foundations of Computer Security* (Springer Science & Business Media 2006)

Sanders A, Young R and Burton M, *Criminal Justice* (Oxford University Press 2010)

Scharre P, *Robotics on the Battlefield – Part 1: Range, Persistence and Daring* (Center for a New American Security, 2014)

Schleifer R, Davis RC and Mergler N, *Culture and Cognition: The Boundaries of Literary and Scientific Inquiry* (Cornell University Press 1992)

Searle JR, *Consciousness and Language* (Cambridge University Press 2002)

Searle JR, *The Mystery of Consciousness* (The New York Review of Books 1997)

Shaikh TN and Agrawal SA, *Engineering Cotton Yarns with Artificial Neural Networking (ANN)* (1st edn, WPI Publishing 5th December 2017)

Shear J, *Explaining Consciousness: The Hard Problem* (MIT Press 1999)

Shershow SC, *Deconstructing Dignity A Critique of the Right-to-Die Debate* (The University of Chicago Press 2014)

Shettleworth SJ, *Cognition, Evolution, and Behavior* (2nd edn, Oxford University Press 2010)

Siegel L, *Essentials of Criminal Justice* (Cengage Learning 2008)

Slade S, *Artificial Intelligence Applications on Wall Street* (1st edn, Routledge 30th November 2017)

Smillie G, *Analogue and Digital Communication Techniques* (Elsevier Science 1999)

Sparks R, *The SAGE Handbook of Punishment and Society* (SAGE 2012)

Stark J, *A Death of One's Own: Literature, Law, and the Right to Die* (Northwestern University Press 2018)

Steele J, *Tort Law: Text, Cases, and Materials* (3rd edn, Oxford University Press 2014)

Sternberg RJ and Kaufman JC, *The Evolution of Intelligence* (Lawrence Erlbaum Associates 2002)

Sutton RS and Barto AG, *Reinforcement Learning: An Introduction* (MIT Press 2018)

Thornton JE and Winkler ER, *Ethics and Aging: The Right to Live, The Right to Die* (The University of British Columbia 1988)

Tirri K and Nokelainen P, *Measuring Multiple Intelligences and Moral Sensitivities in Education* (Sense Publishers 2011)

Trent JW, *Inventing the Feeble Mind: A History of Intellectual Disability in the United States* (Oxford University Press 2017)

Tulich T and others, *Regulating Preventive Justice: Principle, Policy and Paradox* (Routledge 2017)

Turner J, *Robot Rules: Regulating Artificial Intelligence* (Springer 2018)

Uttal WR, *Dualism: The Original Sin of Cognitivism* (Lawrence Erlbaum Associates 2004)

Velmans M, *Understanding Consciousness* (1st edn, Routledge 11th September 2002)

Věra Kůrková and others, *Artificial Neural Networks and Machine Learning – ICANN 2018: 27th International Conference on Artificial Neural Networks, Rhodes, Greece, October 4-7, 2018, Proceedings, Part 3* (Springer 2018)

Warwick K, *Artificial Intelligence: The Basics* (1st edn, Routledge 1st March 2013)

Weitzenfeld A, Arbib M and Alexander A, *The Neural Simulation Language: A System for Brain Modelling* (Massachusetts Institute of Technology 2002)

Whiting R, *A Natural Right to Die: Twenty-Three Centuries of Debate* (Greenwood Press 2002)

Wood WB, *The Nematode Caenorhabditis elegans* (Cold Spring Harbor Press 1988)

Yount L, *Right to Die and Euthanasia* (Infobase 2007)

Zeng Z and Wang J, *Advances in Neural Network Research and Applications* (Springer-Verlag Berlin Heidelberg 2010)

Zenil H, *A Computable Universe: Understanding and Exploring Nature as Computation* (World Scientific Publishing 2013)

Zetter K, *Countdown to Zero Day: Stuxnet and the Launch of the World's First Digital Weapon* (Crown, 2014)

Zheng N and Xue J, *Statistical Learning and Pattern Analysis for Image and Video Processing* (Springer Science & Business Media, 2009)

Zucker MB, *A Documentary History: The Right to Die Debate* (Greenwood Press 1999)


Journal Articles

A Daneels and W Salter, 'What Is SCADA?' (1999) International Conference on Accelerator and Large Experimental Physics Control Systems 339

A Shademan and others, 'Supervised autonomous robotic soft tissue surgery' [2016] 8(337) Sci Transl Med 337

Abdul Paliwala, 'Rediscovering artificial intelligence and law: an adequate jurisprudence?' [2016] 30(3) International Review of Law Computers and Technology 107

Adam Jackson, 'Sexual harm prevention orders: appropriate restrictions on internet access and the use of digital devices' [2018] 82(1) Journal of Criminal Law 11

Ahmad Nehaluddin, 'Hackers' criminal behaviour and laws related to hacking' [2009] 15(7) Computer and Telecommunications Law Review 159

Alan M Turing, 'Computing Machinery and Intelligence' [1950] 49 Mind 433

Alan M Turing, 'On computable numbers, with an application to the entscheidungsproblem' [1936] 42(1) Proceedings of the London Mathematical Society 230

Alan Reed, 'Ex turpi causa and gross negligence manslaughter' [2005] 69(2) Journal of Criminal Law 132

Alan Reed, 'Gross negligence manslaughter and illegal activity' [2005] 150 Criminal Law 1

Albert Bandura, 'Perceived Self-Efficacy in Cognitive Development and Functioning' (1993) 28(2) Educational Psychologist 117

Alexander Sarch, 'Review of Findlay Stark, Culpable Carelessness: Recklessness and Negligence in the Criminal Law' (2017) 4(12) Criminal Law and Philosophy 725

Amos E Dolbear, 'An Educational Allegory' [1899] 50(14) Journal of Education 235

Andreas Kaplan and Michael Haenlein, 'Siri, Siri, in my hand: Who's the fairest in the land? On the interpretations, illustrations, and implications of artificial intelligence' (2019) 62 Business Horizons 15

Andrés Guadamuz, 'The monkey selfie: copyright lessons for originality in photographs and internet jurisdiction' [2016] 5(1) Internet Policy Review 1

Andrew Hugill, 'Introduction: transdisciplinary learning for digital creative practice' (2013) 3(24) Digital Creativity 165

Andrew J Wu, 'From Video Games to Artificial Intelligence: Assigning Copyright Ownership to Works Generated by Increasingly Sophisticated Computer Programs' (1997) 25(1) AIPLA Quarterly Journal 131

Ann W Branscomb, 'Rogue Computer Programs and Computer Rogues: Tailoring the Punishment to Fit the Crime' (1990) 16(1) Rutgers Computer & Tech Law Journal 1

Anne Lodge, 'Gross negligence manslaughter on the cusp: the unprincipled privileging of harm over culpability' [2017] 81(2) The Journal of Criminal Law 125

B A Rich, 'Personhood, patienthood, and clinical practice: Reassessing advance directives' (1998) 4 Psychology, Public Policy and Law 610

Barry Mitchell, 'Minding the Gap in Unlawful and Dangerous Act Manslaughter: A Moral Defence of One-Punch Killers' (2008) 6(72) The Journal of Criminal Law 537

Brent Kesler, 'The Vulnerability of Nuclear Facilities to Cyber Attack' [2011] 10(1) Strategic Insights 15

Burkhard Schafer, 'The future of IP law in an age of artificial intelligence.' [2016] 13(3) Scripted 283

Charlotte A Tschider 'Deus Ex Machina: Regulating Cybersecurity and Intelligence for Patients of the Future' [2018] 5(1) Savannah Law Review 177

Claire Brock, 'Risk, Responsibility and Surgery in the 1890s and Early 1900s' [2013] 57(3) Med Hist 317

Clyde B Vedder, 'Florida Prison Pioneers Academic In-Service Training,' (1954) 1954 Proceedings of the Annual Congress of Correction of the American Prison Association 60

Curtis E Karnow, 'Launch on Warning: Aggressive Defence of Computer Systems' (2005) 1(7) Yale Journal of Law & Technology 88

Daniel Silverstone and Joe Whittle, '"Forget it, Jake. It's Chinatown": the policing of Chinese organised crime in the UK' (2016) 89(1) Pol J 70

David Deutsch, 'Quantum theory, the Church-Turing principle and the universal quantum computer' (1985) A 400 Proceedings of the Royal Society of London 97

Deirdre Golash and James P Lynch, 'Public Opinion, Crime Seriousness, and Sentencing Policy' (1995) 3 (22) American Journal of Criminal Law 703

Doug Hyne, 'Examining the Legal Challenges to the Restriction of Computer Access as a Term of Probation or Supervised Release.' (2002) 2(28) New England Journal on Criminal and Civil Confinement 215

Eike S Reetz and others, 'Test Driven Life Cycle Management for Internet of Things based Services: a Semantic Approach' (2012) The Fourth International Conference on Advances in System Testing and Validation Lifecycle 21

Ejike Ofuonye and James Miller, 'Securing web-clients with instrumented code and dynamic runtime monitoring' (2013) 6(86) The Journal of Systems and Software 1689

Emilio García-Roselló and Others, 'Visual NNet: An Educational ANN's Simulation Environment Reusing Matlab Neural Networks Toolbox' (2011) 10(2) Informatics in Education 225

Emma L. Flett and Jennifer F. Wilson, 'Artificial intelligence: is Johnny 5 alive? Key bits and bytes from the UK's robotics and artificial intelligence inquiry' [2017] 23(3) C.T.L.R. 72

Erwin Schrödinger, 'Die gegenwärtige Situation in der Quantenmechanik' (1935) 23(48) Naturwissenschaften 807

Gabriel Jacobs and Cliona O'Neill, 'On the reliability (or otherwise) of SIC codes' (2003) 3(15) European Business Review 164

Gavin Dingwall and Alisdair A Gillespie, 'Reconsidering the good Samaritan: a duty to rescue?' [2008] 39 Cambrian Law Review 26

Gordon E. Moore, 'Cramming More Components onto Integrated Circuits' (1965) 38(8) Electronics 114

Gualtiero Piccinini, 'Alan Turing and the Mathematical Objection' (2003) 13(1) Minds and Machines 23

Gualtiero Piccinini, 'Alan Turing and the Mathematical Objection' [2003] 13(1) Minds and Machines 23

Helen Bain, 'Raybould v T&N Gilmartin (Contractors) Ltd: when can the defence of volenti non fit injuria apply?' [2019] 145 Civil Practice Bulletin

Henry T Greely, 'Neuroscience and Criminal Justice: Not Responsibility but Treatment' (2008) 56(5) Kansas Law Review 1103

Howard Gordon, 'The Multivendor Muddle: Heterogeneous local-area networks face proprietary road blocks.' [1986] 35(3) Network World 43

Ian A Elliot, Donald Findlater and Teresa Hughes, 'Practice report: A review of e-Safety remote' (2010) 16(2) Journal of Sexual Aggression 237

James A Jones, Mark Grechanik and Andre van der Hoek, 'Enabling and Enhancing Collaborations between Software Development Organizations and Independent Test Agencies' (2009) ICSE Workshop on Cooperative and Human Aspects on Software Engineering 56

James P Farwell and Rafal Rohozinski, 'Stuxnet and the Future of Cyber War' (2011) 53(1) Survival 23

Jan Engelstädter, 'Asexual but Not Clonal: Evolutionary Processes in Automictic Populations' [2017] 206(2) GENETICS 993

Jeremy Horder, 'Strict liability, statutory construction, and the spirit of liberty' [2002] 118(Jul) Law Quarterly Review 458

Jiahong Chen and Paul Burgess, 'The boundaries of legal personhood: how spontaneous intelligence can problematise differences between humans, artificial intelligence, companies and animals' (March 2019) 27(1) Artificial Intelligence and Law 73

John Demme and others, 'On the Feasibility of Online Malware Detection with Performance Counters' (2013) 3(41) ACM SIGARCH Computer Architecture News 559

John King Gamble, 'Human-Centric International Law: A Model and a Search for Empirical Indicators' [2005] 14 Tulane Journal of International and Comparative Law 61

John McCarthy, 'Programs with Common Sense' [1968] Semantic Information Processing, 403

John R. Searle, 'Minds, Brains, and Programs' [1980] 3(3) Behavioral and Brain Sciences 417

Joseph Lee, 'Shareholders' derivative claims under the Companies Act 2006: market mechanism or asymmetric paternalism?' [2007] 18(11) International Company and Commercial Law Review 378

Joy Macknight, 'The new age of AI fraud detection.' [2017] Oct Banker 40

Judith M Collins and Murray R Clark, 'An Application of the Theory of Neural Computation to the Prediction of Workplace Behavior: An Illustration and Assessment of Network Analysis' (1993) 3(46) Personnel Psychology 503

JW Dornseiffen, 'Residue aspects of disinfectants used in the food industry' (1998) 41(3-4) International Biodeterioration & Biodegradation 309

Katharine Stephens and Tony Bond, 'Artificial intelligence: navigating the IP challenges' [2018] 29(6) PLC Magazine 39

L Nancy Birnbaum, 'Strict Products Liability and Computer Software' (1988) 2(8) Computer Law Journal 135

Lars J Kangas and others, 'Computer-aided tracking and characterization of homicides and sexual assaults (CATCH)' (1999) Proc SPIE 3722, Applications and Science of Computational Intelligence II

Leslie de Chernatony and Francesca Dall'Olmo Riley, 'The chasm between managers' and consumers' views of brands: the experts' perspectives' (1997) 2(5) Journal of Strategic Marketing 89

Loes van Aken and others, 'Representation of the Cattell–Horn–Carroll Theory of Cognitive Abilities in the Factor Structure of the Dutch-Language Version of the WAIS-IV' (2017) 24(4) Assessment 458

Louise Amoore, 'Risk before justice: when the law contests its own suspension' [2008] 21(4) Leiden Journal of International Law 847

M Geistfeld 'Scientific Uncertainty and Causation in Tort Law.' (2001) 3(54) Vanderbilt Law Review 1011

Margaret Brazier and Amel Alghrani, 'Fatal medical malpractice and criminal liability' [2009] 25(2) P.N. 51

Mary Ford, 'The Personhood Paradox and the 'Right to Die" [2005] 13(1) Med. L. Rev. 80

Matt Byrne, 'Fraud watchdog enters brave new world of AI innovation.' [2018] Oct Lawyer 8

Matthew J Conigliaro, Andrew C Greenberg and Mark A Lemley, 'Foreseeability in Patent Law' (2001) 3(16) Berkeley Technology Law Journal 1045

Melih Abdulhayoglu, 'The Need for a United Industry in Combating Malware' (2009) 9 Computer Fraud & Security 5

Michael T. Battista, 'Formal Axiomatic Systems and Computer-Generated Theorems' [1982] 75(3) The Mathematics Teacher 215, 252

Michael Wheeler, 'Plastic Machines: Behavioural Diversity and the Turing Test' [2010] 39(3) Kybernetes 466

MY Rafiq, G Bugmann and DJ Easterbrook, 'Neural network design for engineering applications' (2001) 17(79) Computers and Structures 1541

Nadia N Sawicki, 'Judging Doctors: The Person and the Professional' [2011] 10(13) AMA Journal of Ethics 718

Nature, 'Shock and law: The Italian system's contempt for its scientists' [2012] 490 Nature 446

Neil L Sobol, 'Fighting Fines & Fees: Borrowing from Consumer Law to Combat Criminal Justice Debt Abuses' (2017) 17-34 (88) University of Colorado Law Review 841

Nick Barnard, 'Culpability and mitigation' (2016) 180(2) Criminal Law & Justice Weekly

Nick Bostrom, 'The superintelligent will: Motivation and instrumental rationality in advanced artificial agents.' (2012) 22(2) Minds and Machines 71

Parag C Pendharkara, James A Rodgerb and Girish H Subramanian, 'An empirical study of the Cobb–Douglas production function properties of software development effort' (2008) 50(12) Information and Software Technology 1181

Paul Bratley and Jean Millo, 'Computer recreations' [1972] 2 Software Practice and Experience 397

Paul Wood and Paul Englert, 'Intelligence Compensation Theory: A Critical Examination of the Negative Relationship Between Conscientiousness and Fluid and Crystallised Intelligence' (2009) 2 The Australian and New Zealand Journal of Organisational Psychology 19

Phillip L Ackerman and Margaret E Beier, 'Intelligence, Personality, and Interests in the Career Choice Process' (2003) 11(2) Journal of Career Assessment 205

Pratap Devarapalli, 'Machine learning to machine owning: redefining the copyright ownership from the perspective of Australian, US, UK and EU law' [2018] 40(11) European Interlectual Property Review 722

Rachel Herron, 'A social systems approach to understanding the racial effect of the section 44 counter-terror stop and search powers' [2015] 11(4) Int. J.L.C. 383

Rex E Jung and Richard J Haier, 'The Parieto-Frontal Integration Theory (P-FIT) of intelligence: Converging neuroimaging evidence' (2007) 30(2) Behavioral and Brain Sciences 135

Richard S Frase, 'Punishment Purposes.' (2005) 1(58) Stanford Law Review 67

Russ Shafer-Landau, 'Liberalism and paternalism' [2005] 11(3) Legal Theory 169

Sanjana Kapila, 'A glimpse into the future.' [2018] 278 Managing Intellectual Property 30

Sarah P. Otto and Thomas Lenormand, 'Resolving the paradox of sex and recombination' [2002] 3 Nature Reviews Genetics 252

Scott Zoldi, 'Tin ears - machine learning set against social engineering.' [2018] Oct/Nov Fraud intelligence 21

Sharmeen Lotia and Mark C Bellamy, 'Anaesthesia and morbid obesity' [2008] 8(5) Continuing Education in Anaesthesia Critical Care & Pain 151

SM Solaiman, 'Liability for industrial manslaughter caused by robots under statutory laws in Australia' [2017] 38(7) Company Law 226

Steve Tombs, 'Still killing with impunity: corporate criminal law reform in the UK' (2013) 2(11) Policy and Practice in Health and Safety 63

Steven Goldberg, 'The Changing Face of Death: Computers, Consciousness, and Nancy Cruzan' (1991) 43(3) Stanford Law Review 659

Steven Hutchinson, 'Countering catastrophic criminology: Reform, punishment and the modern liberal compromise' (2006) 4(8) Punishment & Society 443

Stuart J Ritchie, Tucker-Drob and Elliot M, 'How much does education improve intelligence? A meta-analysis' [2018] 29(8) Psychological Science 1358

Stuart Russell, Daniel Dewey and Max Tegmark, 'Research Priorities for Robust and Beneficial Artificial Intelligence' (2015) 4(36) AI Magazine 105

Suzana Herculano-Houzel, 'The Human Brain in Numbers: A Linearly Scaled-up Primate Brain' [2009] 31(3) Frontiers in Human Neuroscience 7

Szilvassy SJ and others, 'Quantitative assay for totipotent reconstituting hematopoietic stem cells by a competitive repopulation strategy.' [1990] 87 Proc. Natl. Acad. Sci. 8736

TE James, 'The Age of Majority' (1960) 4(1) American Journal of Legal History 22

Thomas F Gordon, 'An abductive theory of legal issues' 1 (1991) 35 International Journal of Man-Machine Studies 95

Thomas H Spotts, 'Discriminating Factors in Faculty Use of Instructional Technology on Higher Education' (1999) 2(4) Educational Technology & Society 92

Velmer S Burton and others, 'The Collateral Consequences of a Felony Conviction: A National Study of State Statutes' (1987) 51(3) Federal probation 52

William O Hochkammer, 'Capital Punishment Controversy' (1970) 60(3) Journal of Criminal Law and Criminology 360

Working Papers

Aaron S Gross, 'Religion and Animals' (2017) Oxford Handbooks Online <http://www.oxfordhandbooks.com/view/10.1093/oxfordhb/97801 99935420.001.0001/oxfordhb-9780199935420-e-10?print=pdf> accessed 07 March 2019

Barret Zoph and others, 'Learning Transferable Architectures for Scalable Image Recognition' (2018) Arxiv <https://arxiv.org/pdf/1707.07012.pdf> accessed 15 March 2019

Christian Szegedy and others, 'Going Deeper with Convolutions' [2014] Google Inc <https://arxiv.org/pdf/1409.4842.pdf> accessed 20 April 2019

Dario Amodei and others, 'Concrete Problems in AI Safety' (2016) Google Brain <https://arxiv.org/pdf/1606.06565.pdf> accessed 01 February 2018

Dave Anderson and George McNeill, 'A DACS State-of-the-Art Report: Artificial Neural Networks Technology' (1992) DACS <https://knn.es/Artificial%20Neural%20Network%20Technologie s.pdf> accessed 11 March 2019

Gerard Briscoe and Paolo Dini, 'Towards Autopoietic Computing' [2010] London School of Economics and Political Science <https://arxiv.org/pdf/1009.0797.pdf> accessed 29 April 2019

Home Office, 'Reforming the Law on Involuntary Manslaughter: The Government's Proposals' (2000) Home Office Government Proposal Paper May 2000

<http://www.corporateaccountability.org.uk/dl/manslaughter/refor
m/archive/homeofficedraft2000.pdf> accessed 27 April 2019

iPullRank, 'Machine Learning for Marketers: A Comprehensive
Guide to Machine Learning' (2017) iPullRank
<https://assets.ctfassets.net/j5zy0n17n2ql/2D4mX8PjV6iC6i8clu
SCwk/23a4ebb99a6e9d5a82b2f03e1262f39d/ml-
whitepaper.pdf> accessed 06 March 2019

Jack Copeland, 'The Mathematical Objection: Turing, Gödel, and
Penrose on the Mind' (2008) Donald Bren School of Information
and Computer Sciences
<https://www.ics.uci.edu/~welling/teaching/271fall09/Copeland---
TheMathematicalObjection.pdf> accessed 15 March 2019

Joel Lehman and others, 'The Surprising Creativity of Digital
Evolution: A Collection of Anecdotes from the Evolutionary
Computation and Artificial Life Research Communities' [2018]
Cornell University Neural and Evolutionary Computing
arXiv:1803.03453v1 <https://arxiv.org/abs/1803.03453v1>
accessed 05 March 2019

Lydia Jackson and Richard Cracknell, 'Road accident casualties
in Britain and the world' (2018) Commons Briefing Papers CBP-
7615
<https://researchbriefings.parliament.uk/ResearchBriefing/Summ
ary/CBP-7615#fullreport> accessed 18 April 2019

Mathias Lechner, Radu Grosu, Ramin M. Hasani, 'Worm-level
Control through Search-based Reinforcement Learning' (6th
February 2018) Technische Universität Wien

<https://www.tuwien.ac.at/en/news/news_detail/article/125597/>
accessed 02 December 2018

Miles Brundage and others, 'The malicious use of artificial
intelligence: Forecasting prevention and mitigation' (2018)
University of Oxford
<https://arxiv.org/ftp/arxiv/papers/1802/1802.07228.pdf>
accessed 10 April 2019

Ministry of Defence, A Soldier's Guide to the Law of Armed
Conflict (2005) Document Number AC71130
<https://assets.publishing.service.gov.uk/government/uploads/sy
stem/uploads/attachment_data/file/619906/2017-04714.pdf>
accessed 10 November 2018

Nelson Fernandez, Carlos Maldonado, Carlos Gershenson,
'Information Measures of Complexity, Emergence, Self-
organization, Homeostasis, and Autopoiesis' (31st July 2013)
Univesidad de Pamplona <https://arxiv.org/abs/1304.1842>
accessed 01 November 2018

Oscar Chang, Hod Lipson, 'Neural Network Quine' (24th May
2018) Columbia University <https://arxiv.org/abs/1803.05859>
accessed 02 November 2018

T Ishida, Y Sasaki and Y Fukuhara, 'Use of procedural
programming languages for controlling production systems'
[1991] IEEE
<https://ieeexplore.ieee.org/stamp/stamp.jsp?tp=&arnumber=12
0848> accessed 15 March 2019

University of British Columbia, 'The 80386SX Processor Bus and Real-Mode Instruction Set' [2000] EECE 379: design of digital and microcomputer systems <http://www.ece.ubc.ca/~edc/379/lectures/lec2.pdf> accessed 04 November 2018

University of Chicago, 'Fundamental Issues in Machine Learning' (2009) The University of Chicago <https://ttic.uchicago.edu/~pengjian/MLCourse/intro.pdf> accessed 06 March 2019

Vyara Apostolova, 'Acts and Statutory Instruments: the volume of UK legislation 1950 to 2016' (2017) Commons Briefing Papers CBP-7438 <https://researchbriefings.parliament.uk/ResearchBriefing/Summary/CBP-7438#fullreport> accessed 27 April 2019

Vyas Ajay Bhagwat, 'Deep Learning for Chatbots' (2018) San Jose University Masters Projects <https://scholarworks.sjsu.edu/cgi/viewcontent.cgi?article=1645&context=etd_projects> accessed 05 March 2019

Conferences

Stanley James, 'Philosophy of AI: David Chalmers and the Hard Problem of Consciousness' (Mindbuilding Seminar, University of Osnabrück, 2003)

Insight

Daniel Greenberg, 'Joint enterprise', Insight (16 August 2018) <Westlaw> accessed 18 April 2019

Greenberg, 'Strict liability (criminal)', Insight (11 January 2019) <Westlaw> accessed 28 April 2019

Ian Meikle, 'Foreseeability', Insight (10 July 2018) <Westlaw> accessed 20 April 2019

Westlaw UK, 'Health and safety: regulation and enforcement', Insight (26 June 2018) <Westlaw> accessed 04 March 2019


Religious Texts

*The King James Bible* (1611)

*The Quran*


Websites

!MEDIENGRUPPE BITNIK, 'Random DarkNet Shopper' (!MEDIENGRUPPE BITNIK, 14th October 2014) <https://wwwwwwwwwwwwwwwwwwwwwwww.bitnik.org/r/> accessed 28 February 2018

Aatif Sulleyman, 'AI is highly likely to destroy humans, Elon Musk warns' (The Independent, 24th November 2017) <https://www.independent.co.uk/life-style/gadgets-and-tech/news/elon-musk-artificial-intelligence-openai-neuralink-ai-warning-a8074821.html> accessed 08 October 2018

Aatif Sulleyman, 'Google AI creates its own 'Child' AI that's more advanced than Systems built by Humans' (The Independent, 5th December 2017) < https://www.independent.co.uk/life-style/gadgets-and-tech/news/google-child-ai-bot-nasnet-automl-machine-learning-artificial-intelligence-a8093201.html> accessed 13 November 2018

Aatif Sulleyman, 'Google AI creates its own 'Child' AI that's more advanced than Systems built by Humans' (The Independent, 5th December 2017) <https://www.independent.co.uk/life-style/gadgets-and-tech/news/google-child-ai-bot-nasnet-automl-machine-learning-artificial-intelligence-a8093201.html> accessed 13 November 2018

ACRO, 'Managing more sex offender records than ever before' (ACRO, 5th September 2018) <https://www.acro.police.uk/acro_std.aspx?id=2288> accessed 28 April 2019

Adam Conner-Simons and Rachel Gordon, 'Teaching machines to predict the future' (MIT News, 21st June 2016) <http://news.mit.edu/2016/teaching-machines-to-predict-the-future-0621> accessed 15 March 2019

Alex Hern, 'Google's Go-playing AI still undefeated with victory over world number one' (The Guardian, 25th May 2017) <https://www.theguardian.com/technology/2017/may/25/alphago-google-ai-victory-world-go-number-one-china-ke-jie> accessed 28 February 2018

Alexis Ulrich, 'Long and short numeric scales' (Of Language and Numbers, 24th August 2013)

<https://www.languagesandnumbers.com/articles/en/long-and-short-numeric-scales/> accessed 30 November 2018

Amazon, 'AMD FX 8350 Black Edition "Vishera" CPU (8 Core, AM3+, Clock 4.0 GHz, Turbo 4.2 GHz, 8 MB L3 Cache, 125 W)' (Amazon.co.uk, 22nd April 2014) <http://amzn.eu/d/hanfQom> accessed 12 October 2018

Amazon, 'Intel i7-7700K Quad Core 4.2GHz LGA1151 HD 630 8MB Intel HD Graphics Cache 91W TDP CPU Processor' (Amazon.co.uk, 23rd October 2012) <https://www.amazon.co.uk/Intel-i7-7700K-LGA1151-Graphics-Processor/dp/B01LTI1JEM/> accessed 13 October 2018

American GO Association, 'A Brief History of Go' (American GO Association, 2019) <http://www.usgo.org/brief-history-go> accessed 11 March 2019

Andres Guadamuz, 'Artificial intelligence and copyright' (World Intellectual Property Organisation, October 2017) <https://www.wipo.int/wipo_magazine/en/2017/05/article_0003.html> accessed 16 March 2019

Andrés Guadamuz, 'Can the monkey selfie case teach us anything about copyright law?' (World Intellectual Property Magazine, February 2018) <https://www.wipo.int/wipo_magazine/en/2018/01/article_0007.html> accessed 10 March 2019

Ashley Deeks, 'Diplomatic immunity protects even Erdogan's thugs. We have to live with that.' (The Washington Post, 18th May 2017)

<https://www.washingtonpost.com/posteverything/wp/2017/05/18
/diplomatic-immunity-protects-all-officials-even-erdogans-thugs-
thats-good/?noredirect=on&utm_term=.9fd8c4d89e82>
accessed 26 April 2019

Barret Zoph and others, 'AutoML for large scale image
classification and object detection' (Google AI Blog, 2nd
November 2017) <https://ai.googleblog.com/2017/11/automl-for-
large-scale-image.html> accessed 15 March 2019

BBC News, 'A Point of View: Will machines ever be able to
think?' (BBC News, 13th October 2013)
<https://www.bbc.co.uk/news/magazine-24565995> accessed 02
December 2018

Benjamin Bathke, 'Artificial intelligence, or the end of the world
as we know it' (Deutsche Welle, 26th October 2018)
<https://www.dw.com/cda/en/artificial-intelligence-ai-automation-
technology-harari-machine-learning-ethics-obama-future-oslo/a-
45932260> accessed 14 April 2019

Bernard Marr, 'How AI and Machine Learning are transforming
Law Firms and the Legal Sector' (Forbes, 23rd May 2018)
<https://www.forbes.com/sites/bernardmarr/2018/05/23/how-ai-
and-machine-learning-are-transforming-law-firms-and-the-legal-
sector/> accessed 06 July 2018

BIPM, 'SI Brochure: The International System of Units (SI) [8th
edition, 2006; updated in 2014]' (BIPM, 1st February 2001)
<https://www.bipm.org/en/publications/si-brochure/second.html>
accessed 13 March 2019

Cal Jeffrey, 'Machine-learning algorithm beats 20 lawyers in NDA legal analysis' (TechSpot, 31st October 2018) <https://www.techspot.com/news/77189-machine-learning-algorithm-beats-20-lawyers-nda-legal.html> accessed 27 April 2019

Chris Lobanov-Rostovsky, 'Chapter 8: Sex Offender Management Strategies' (Sex Offender Management Assessment and Planning Initiative, 24th October 2014) <https://www.smart.gov/SOMAPI/sec1/ch8_strategies.html> accessed 28 April 2019

Chris Skidmore, 'Adrian Smith Review:Written statement - HCWS1449' (Parliament, 26th March 2019) <https://www.parliament.uk/business/publications/written-questions-answers-statements/written-statement/Commons/2019-03-26/HCWS1449/> accessed 29 April 2019

Chris Woodford, 'Computers' (ExplainThatStuff, 25th December 2019) <https://www.explainthatstuff.com/howcomputerswork.html> accessed 06 April 2019

CISCO, 'What Is the Difference: Viruses, Worms, Trojans, and Bots?' (Cisco Systems, 14th June 2018) <https://www.cisco.com/c/en/us/about/security-center/virus-differences.html#3> accessed 06 April 2019

Claudia Hammond, 'Do we only use 10% of our brains?' (BBC Future, 13th November 2012)

<http://www.bbc.com/future/story/20121112-do-we-only-use-10-of-our-brains> accessed 30 November 2018

Comodo, 'Anti-Malware Database' (Comodo, 21st October 2011) <https://www.comodo.com/home/internet-security/updates/vdp/database.php> accessed 29 April 2019

Crown Prosecution Service, 'Homicide: Murder and Manslaughter' (Crown Prosecution Service, 19 February 2019) <https://www.cps.gov.uk/legal-guidance/homicide-murder-and-manslaughter> accessed 04 March 2019

DeepMind, 'DeepMind' (DeepMind Technologies Limited, 2018) <https://deepmind.com/> accessed 28 February 2018

Dejure, 'Urheberrechtsgesetz' (Dejure, 19th March 2019) <https://dejure.org/gesetze/UrhG/7.html> accessed 19 March 2019

Demis Hassabis and David Silver, 'AlphaGo Zero: Learning from scratch' (DeepMind, 18th October 2017) <https://deepmind.com/blog/alphago-zero-learning-scratch/> accessed 1 December 2018

Emerging Technology, 'When an AI finally kills someone, who will be responsible?' (MIT Technology Review, 12th March 2018) <https://www.technologyreview.com/s/610459/when-an-ai-finally-kills-someone-who-will-be-responsible/> accessed 14 April 2019

Ethan Siegel, 'Can Science Prove the Existence of God?' (Forbes, 20th January 2017) <https://www.forbes.com/sites/startswithabang/2017/01/20/can-science-prove-the-existence-of-god/> accessed 14 March 2019

Facebook Newsroom, 'Stats' (Facebook.com, 31st March 2019) <https://newsroom.fb.com/company-info/> accessed 28 April 2019

Facebook, 'Facebook' (Facebook.Com, 28th April 2019) <https://www.facebook.com/> accessed 28 April 2019

Financial Conduct Authority, 'Financial Conduct Authority' (FCA, 29th April 2019) <https://www.fca.org.uk/> accessed 29 April 2019

Francesca Bria, 'The robot economy may already have arrived' (Open Democracy, 20th February 2016) <https://www.opendemocracy.net/en/can-europe-make-it/robot-economy-full-automation-work-future/> accessed 15 March 2019

George Dvorsky, 'Breakthrough: The First Complete Computer Model of a Living Organism' (Gizmodo Biology, 23rd July 2012) <https://io9.gizmodo.com/breakthrough-the-first-complete-computer-model-of-a-li-5928218> accessed 06 April 2019

George Seif, 'AutoKeras: The Killer of Google's AutoML' (Towards Data Science, 31st July 2018) <https://towardsdatascience.com/autokeras-the-killer-of-googles-automl-9e84c552a319> accessed 05 March 2019

GOV.UK, 'The Highway Code' (GOV.UK, 1st October 2015) <https://www.gov.uk/guidance/the-highway-code> accessed 22 December 2018

Gunnar Schulze, 'Neural Networks, Brain Bugs and Deep Learning' (Norbis, 20th June 2016)

<https://norbis.w.uib.no/blog/neural-networks-brain-bugs-and-deep-learning/> accessed 29 April 2019

Hannah Summers, 'Uber suspends fleet of self-driving cars following Arizona crash' (The Guardian, 26th March 2017) <https://www.theguardian.com/technology/2017/mar/26/uber-suspends-self-driving-cars-arizona-crash-volvo-suv> accessed 13 April 2019

Hardware Museum, 'AMD AM386 DXL-40' (Hardware Museum, 28th November 2018) <http://hw-museum.cz/cpu/130/amd-am386-dxl-40> accessed 02 December 2018

Hawkins Spizman Fortas, 'Are Parents Responsible for Children's Crimes?' (Hawkins Spizman Fortas, 20th December 2018) <https://www.hsflawfirm.com/are-parents-responsible-for-childrens-crimes/> accessed 20 April 2019

Health and Safety Executive, 'Identify the hazards' (Health and Safety Executive, 8th April 2019) <http://www.hse.gov.uk/risk/identify-the-hazards.htm> accessed 15 April 2019

Helen Coffey, 'UK Drivers spend £4bn repairing car damage caused by potholes each year' (The Independent, 9th April 2019) <https://www.independent.co.uk/travel/news-and-advice/potholes-spend-uk-drivers-cost-damaged-roads-a8861376.html> accessed 13 April 2019

Ian Sample, "It's able to create knowledge itself': Google unveils AI that learns on its own' (Guardian, 18th October 2017) <https://www.theguardian.com/science/2017/oct/18/its-able-to-

create-knowledge-itself-google-unveils-ai-learns-all-on-its-own>
accessed 15 March 2019

Ian Sample, 'Thousands of leading AI researchers sign pledge against killer robots' (Guardian, 18th July 2018) <https://www.theguardian.com/science/2018/jul/18/thousands-of-scientists-pledge-not-to-help-build-killer-ai-robots> accessed 06 April 2019

Intel, 'Intel at 50: Gordon Moore on the Founding of Intel' (Intel News Byte, 2nd July 2018) <https://newsroom.intel.com/news/intel-50-gordon-moore-founding-intel/> accessed 30 November 2018

Intel, 'Intel® Celeron® Processor 800 MHz, 128K Cache, 100 MHz FSB' (Intel Support, January 2001) <https://ark.intel.com/products/27197/Intel-Celeron-Processor-800-MHz-128K-Cache-100-MHz-FSB> accessed 01 December 2018

Intel, 'Intel® Core™ i5-750 Processor' (Intel Support, September 2009) <https://ark.intel.com/products/42915/Intel-Core-i5-750-Processor-8M-Cache-2-66-GHz-> accessed 01 December 2018

Intel, 'Intel® Core™ I9-7980XE Extreme Edition Processor' (Intel, August 2017) <https://www.intel.co.uk/content/www/uk/en/products/processors/core/x-series/i9-7980xe.html> accessed 02 December 2018

Intel, 'Intel® Pentium® Processor 150 MHz, 60 MHz FSB' (Intel Support, November 1995)

<https://ark.intel.com/products/49958/Intel-Pentium-Processor-150-MHz-60-MHz-FSB> accessed 01 December 2018

Intel, 'The Story of the Intel® 4004: Intel's First Microprocessor' (Intel, Unknown Date) <https://www.intel.co.uk/content/www/uk/en/history/museum-story-of-intel-4004.html> accessed 03 November 2018

Jacob Devlin and Ming-Wei Chang, 'Open Sourcing BERT: State-of-the-Art Pre-training for Natural Language Processing' (Google AI Blog, 2nd November 2018) <https://ai.googleblog.com/2018/11/open-sourcing-bert-state-of-art-pre.html> accessed 13 November 2018

James Vincent, 'Tencent says there are only 300,000 AI engineers worldwide, but millions are needed' (The Verge, 5th December 2017) <https://www.theverge.com/2017/12/5/16737224/global-ai-talent-shortfall-tencent-report> accessed 27 April 2019

James Warrington, 'Hacker stereotypes exacerbate UK's cyber security skills shortage, warns NCSC' (City AM, 11th February 2019) <http://www.cityam.com/273066/computer-geek-stereotypes-causing-cyber-security-skills> accessed 25 April 2019

Jason M Rubin, 'Can a computer generate a truly random number?' (MIT School of Engineering, 1st November 2011) <https://engineering.mit.edu/engage/ask-an-engineer/can-a-computer-generate-a-truly-random-number/> accessed 15 March 2019

Jeff Dunn, 'Here are the companies that sell the most PCs worldwide' (Business Insider, 14th April 2017) <https://www.businessinsider.com/top-pc-companies-sales-idc-market-share-chart-2017-4?r=US&IR=T> accessed 27 April 2019

Jens Stoltenberg, 'The Three Ages of NATO: An Evolving Alliance' (NATO, 23rd September 2016) <https://www.nato.int/cps/en/natohq/opinions_135317.htm?selectedLocale=en> accessed 01 March 2018

Jesse Miller, 'Computer Tools | Computer Features & Benefits' (streetdirectory.com, 2019) <https://www.streetdirectory.com/travel_guide/136883/computers/computer_tools__computer_features__benefits.html> accessed 05 March 2019

Jesus Rodriguez, 'Machine Learning for Detecting Code Bugs' (Towards Data Science, 11 February 2019) <https://towardsdatascience.com/machine-learning-for-detecting-code-bugs-a79f37f144b7> accessed 27 April 2019

John Shook, 'Proving God's Existence Is Impossible So Stop Trying' (Centre for Enquiry, 16th November 2011) <https://centerforinquiry.org/blog/proving_gods_existence_is_impossible/> accessed 14 March 2019

Jori Finkel, 'After a year-long journey in the California desert, Desert X's art rover Shybot is found' (The Art Newspaper, 25th July 2018) <https://www.theartnewspaper.com/news/desert-x-rover-shybot-is-found-in-the-california-desert> accessed 14 October 2018

Jori Finkel, 'Things Go Awry at 'Desert X,' as Shy Bot Disappears' (New York Times, 17th March 2017) <https://www.nytimes.com/2017/03/17/arts/design/desert-x-show-things-go-awry-shy-bot-disappears.html> accessed 14 October 2018

Judy van Rhijn, 'Do strong IP laws stifle innovation?' (Canadian Lawyer, 3rd July 2012) <https://www.canadianlawyermag.com/author/na/do-strong-ip-laws-stifle-innovation-1662/> accessed 27 April 2019

Karen McCandless, 'What is Computer Programming?' (Code Academy, 13th June 2018) <https://news.codecademy.com/what-is-computer-programming/> accessed 29 April 2019

Kenny Eliason, 'Difference between Object-Oriented Programming and Procedural Programming Languages' (NeonBrand, 1st August 2013) <https://neonbrand.com/website-design/procedural-programming-vs-object-oriented-programming-a-review/> accessed 15 March 2019

Larry Greenemeier, 'Seeking Address: Why Cyber Attacks Are So Difficult to Trace Back to Hackers' (Scientific American, 11th June 2011) <https://www.scientificamerican.com/article/tracking-cyber-hackers/> accessed 28 April 2019

Lawrence Rifkin, 'Is the Meaning of Your Life to Make Babies?' (Scientific American, 24th March 2013) <https://blogs.scientificamerican.com/guest-blog/is-the-meaning-of-your-life-to-make-babies/> accessed 13 March 2019

Maggie Koerth-Baker, 'Why Global Hackers Are Nearly Impossible to Catch' (Live Science, 19th June 2008) <https://www.livescience.com/2627-global-hackers-impossible-catch.html> accessed 28 April 2019

Malay Haldar, 'Did Turing Prove Machines Will Never Equal Humans?' (A Medium Corporation, 9th January 2016) <https://medium.com/technology-invention-and-more/did-turing-prove-machines-will-never-equal-humans-d73019b74a55> accessed 05 April 2019

Margaret Rouse, 'multi-core processor' (TechTarget, August 2013) <https://searchdatacenter.techtarget.com/definition/multi-core-processor> accessed 06 March 2019

Massimiliano Versace, 'Does Artificial Intelligence Require Specialized Processors?' (The New Stack, 20th October 2017) <https://thenewstack.io/ai-hardware-software-dilemma/> accessed 27 April 2019

Matthew Griffin, 'IBM injected a virus into a neural net to create an undetectable cyberweapon' (Fanatical Futurist, 27th August 2018) <https://www.fanaticalfuturist.com/2018/08/ibm-created-an-undetectable-cyberweapon-by-injecting-viruses-into-neural-nets/ > accessed 06 April 2019

Michael Lacewing, 'Are all humans persons?' (Routledge, 16th November 2012) <http://cw.routledge.com/textbooks/alevelphilosophy/data/AS/Persons/Arehumanspersons.pdf> accessed 08 March 2019

Michael Spencer, 'Artificial Intelligence Regulation May Be Impossible' (Forbes, 2nd March 2019) <https://www.forbes.com/sites/cognitiveworld/2019/03/02/artificial-intelligence-regulation-will-be-impossible/#42210a9011ed> accessed 27 April 2019

Michaela Ross, 'Tech-Savvy Attorneys in Heavy Demand Amid Emerging Tech' (Bloomberg Law, 22nd February 2018) <https://www.bna.com/techsavvy-attorneys-heavy-n57982089186/> accessed 25 April 2019

Multi-Agency Public Protection Arrangements, '8 ViSOR' (MAPPA Guidance, 5th September 2015) <https://mappa.justice.gov.uk/connect.ti/MAPPA/view?objectId=6854964> accessed 29 April 2019

Nathan Collins, 'How artificial intelligence is changing science' (Stanford News, 15th May 2018) <https://news.stanford.edu/2018/05/15/how-ai-is-changing-science/> accessed 19 April 2019

National Museum of natural History, 'Bigger Brains: Complex Brains for a Complex World' (Smithsonian Institution, 6th March 2019) <http://humanorigins.si.edu/human-characteristics/brains> accessed 06 March 2019

Neel Burton, 'Can It Be Right to Commit Suicide?' (Psychology Today, 22nd May 2012) <https://www.psychologytoday.com/gb/blog/hide-and-seek/201205/can-it-be-right-commit-suicide> accessed 13 March 2019

Nick Barnard, 'Culpability and mitigation – sentencing in medical gross negligence manslaughter' (CorkerBinning, 20th January 2016) <https://www.corkerbinning.com/culpability-and-mitigation-sentencing-in-medical-gross-negligence-manslaughter/> accessed 18 April 2019

Nick Srnicek, '4 Reasons Why Technological Unemployment Might Really Be Different This Time' (Novara Media, 30th March 2015) <https://novaramedia.com/2015/03/30/4-reasons-why-technological-unemployment-might-really-be-different-this-time/> accessed 15 March 2019

NOAA, 'What is LIDAR?' (National Oceanic and Atmospheric Administration, 25th May 2018) <https://oceanservice.noaa.gov/facts/lidar.html> accessed 11 April 2019

Oscar Williams-Grut, 'Robots will steal your job: How AI could increase unemployment and inequality' (Business Insider, 15th February 2016) <https://www.businessinsider.com/robots-will-steal-your-job-citi-ai-increase-unemployment-inequality-2016-2?r=UK&IR=T> accessed 15 March 2019

Parliament, 'Bill documents — Automated and Electric Vehicles Act 2018' (Parliament, 19th July 2018) <https://services.parliament.uk/bills/2017-19/automatedandelectricvehicles/documents.html> accessed 06 March 2019

Parliament, 'What is Secondary Legislation?' (Parliament.gov.uk, 21st July 2018)

<https://www.parliament.uk/about/how/laws/secondary-legislation/> accessed 27 April 2019

PassMark Software, 'CPU Benchmarks: AMD A10-5800K APU' (PassMark Software, October 2012) <https://www.cpubenchmark.net/cpu.php?cpu=AMD+A10-5800K+APU&id=1446> accessed 02 December 2018

Patrick Kelly, 'Preemptive Self-Defense, Customary International Law, and the Congolese Wars' (E-International Relations Students, 3rd September 2016) <https://www.e-ir.info/2016/09/03/preemptive-self-defense-customary-international-law-and-the-congolese-wars/> accessed 28 April 2019Chris Morris, 'Made in Britain: What does it mean for trade after Brexit?' (BBC News, 26th March 2018) <https://www.bbc.co.uk/news/uk-politics-43516496> accessed 27 April 2019

Peter Bradley, 'Turing Test and Machine Intelligence' (The Mind Project, 2002) <http://www.mind.ilstu.edu/curriculum/turing_machines/turing_test_and_machine_intelligence.php> accessed 01 December 2018

Robert Hart, 'If an AI creates a work of art, who owns the copyright?' (World Economic Forum, 16th August 2017) <https://www.weforum.org/agenda/2017/08/if-an-ai-creates-a-work-of-art-who-owns-the-copyright> accessed 16 March 2019

Robert Skidelsky, 'Rise of the robots: what will the future of work look like?' (Guardian, 19th February 2013) <https://www.theguardian.com/business/2013/feb/19/rise-of-robots-future-of-work> accessed 15 March 2019

Robert Wheeler, 'Gross negligence manslaughter: what does 'gross' entail?' (University Hospital Southampton, February 2018) <http://www.uhs.nhs.uk/HealthProfessionals/Clinical-law-updates/Gross-negligence-manslaughter-what-does-gross-entail.aspx> accessed 06 November 2018

Rory Cellan-Jones, 'Stephen Hawking warns artificial intelligence could end mankind' (BBC, 2nd December 2014) <https://www.bbc.co.uk/news/technology-30290540> accessed 08 October 2018

Rosalind W. Picard, 'ShyBot' (MIT, 2007) <https://www.media.mit.edu/projects/shybot/overview/> accessed 14 October 2018

Russell Howard Tuttle, 'Human evolution' (Encyclopaedia Britannica, 8th January 2019) <https://www.britannica.com/science/human-evolution> accessed 06 March 2019

Sam Levin, 'Uber crash shows 'catastrophic failure' of self-driving technology, experts say' (The Guardian, 22nd March 2018) <https://www.theguardian.com/technology/2018/mar/22/self-driving-car-uber-death-woman-failure-fatal-crash-arizona> accessed 03 December 2018

Sandro Villinger, 'How powerful a computer do you really need?' (AVG, 16th July 2018) <https://www.avg.com/en/signal/how-powerful-a-computer-do-you-really-need> accessed 05 March 2019

Scott Graham, 'No Standing for Monkey to Bring Selfie Copyright Suit' (The Recorder, 23rd April 2018) <https://www.law.com/therecorder/2018/04/23/no-standing-for-monkey-to-bring-selfie-copyright-suit/?slreturn=20190209214241> accessed 10 March 2019

Sean Gallagher, 'Gears of war: When mechanical analog computers ruled the waves' (ARS Technica, 18th March 2014) <https://arstechnica.com/information-technology/2014/03/gears-of-war-when-mechanical-analog-computers-ruled-the-waves/> accessed 19 March 2019

Security Industry Authority, 'Licence Conditions' (SIA, 1st March 2018) <https://www.sia.homeoffice.gov.uk/Pages/licensing-conditions.aspx> accessed 29 April 2019

Security Industry Authority, 'Licensable Roles' (SIA, 12th July 2018) <https://www.sia.homeoffice.gov.uk/Pages/licensing-roles.aspx> accessed 29 April 2019

Security Industry Authority, 'Security Industry Authority' (SIA, 29th April 2019) <https://www.sia.homeoffice.gov.uk/Pages/home.aspx> accessed 29 April 2019

Sentencing Council, 'Sentencing guidelines for manslaughter introduced' (Sentencing Council, 31 July 2018) <https://www.sentencingcouncil.org.uk/news/item/sentencing-guidelines-for-manslaughter-introduced/> accessed 27 April 19

Shehab Khan, 'Self-driving taxis to be launched in London by 2021, Addison Lee says' (The Independent, 22nd October 2018)

<https://www.independent.co.uk/news/uk/home-news/self-driving-taxis-london-addison-lee-ride-sharing-technology-a8595381.html> accessed 20 April 2019

Shelby Rogers, 'Google's AI Now Creates Code Better Than its Creators' (Interesting Engineering, 18th October 2017) <https://interestingengineering.com/googles-ai-now-creates-code-better-than-its-creators> accessed 20 April 2019

Shepherd and Wedderburn LLP, 'Changes to the Computer Misuse Act' (Lexology, 10th December 2008) <https://www.lexology.com/library/detail.aspx?g=84d37161-052e-4c40-b97d-408321679364> accessed 23 April 2019

Stackify, 'Dev Leaders Compare Continuous Delivery vs. Continuous Deployment vs. Continuous Integration' (Stackify, 25th July 2017) <https://stackify.com/continuous-delivery-vs-continuous-deployment-vs-continuous-integration/> accessed 20 April 2019

Stanford Encyclopaedia of Philosophy, 'The Chinese Room Argument' (Stanford Encyclopaedia of Philosophy, 19th March 2004) <https://plato.stanford.edu/entries/chinese-room/#4> accessed 30 November 2018

Stephen Hawking and others, 'Stephen Hawking: 'Transcendence looks at the implications of artificial intelligence - but are we taking AI seriously enough?'' (Independent, 1st May 2014) <https://www.independent.co.uk/news/science/stephen-hawking-transcendence-looks-at-the-implications-of-artificial-intelligence-but-are-we-taking-9313474.html> accessed 14 April 2019

Steve Bullock, 'Brexit is not inevitable. These are the steps Parliament could take to halt it' (The London School of Economics and Political Science, 14th May 2018) <https://blogs.lse.ac.uk/brexit/2018/05/14/brexit-is-not-inevitable-these-are-the-steps-parliament-could-take-to-halt-it/> accessed 15 March 2019

Tammy Webber, 'The death of a college student who got into a car she thought was an Uber could spark a crackdown for ride-hailing safety' (Business Insider, 7th April 2019) <https://www.businessinsider.com/slaying-puts-focus-on-ride-hailing-safety-fake-drivers-2019-4?r=US&IR=T> accessed 29 April 2019

Tanya Lewis, 'Don't Let Artificial Intelligence Take Over, Top Scientists Warn' (Live Science, 12th January 2015) <https://www.livescience.com/49419-artificial-intelligence-dangers-letter.html> accessed 15 March 2019

Techopedia Staff, 'What is the difference between artificial intelligence and neural networks?' (Technopedia, 2nd June 2017) <https://www.techopedia.com/2/27888/programming/what-is-the-difference-between-artificial-intelligence-and-neural-networks> accessed 11 April 2019

Thomas Connelly, 'Sounding the argument against the Turing Test from continuity in the nervous system.' (Philosophy Online, 17th September 2018) <https://philosophyonline.blog/2018/09/17/sounding-the-argument-against-the-turing-test-from-continuity-in-the-nervous-system/> accessed 02 December 2018

Ursula Martin, 'Ada Lovelace and the abstract machine' (The Times Literary Supplement, 11th October 2016) <https://www.the-tls.co.uk/articles/public/ada-lovelaces-abstract-machine/> accessed 05 March 2019

Virtual Box, 'Welcome to VirtualBox.org!' (VirtualBox, 26th September 2011) <https://www.virtualbox.org/manual/ch01.html> accessed 11 March 2019

Waymo, 'Waymo' (Waymo, 5th December 2018) <https://waymo.com/> accessed 06 April 2019

Wayve, 'Learning to drive in a day.' (Wayve Research, 28th June 2018) <https://wayve.ai/blog/learning-to-drive-in-a-day-with-reinforcement-learning> accessed 13 April 2019

Ying Hui Tan, 'Law Report: Child in care cannot sue council: X (minors) v Bedfordshire County Council - Queen's Bench Division (Mr Justice Turner), 12 November 1993' (The Independent, 23 December 1993) <https://www.independent.co.uk/arts-entertainment/law-report-child-in-care-cannot-sue-council-x-minors-v-bedfordshire-county-council-queens-bench-1469142.html> accessed 05 March 2019